PROMISE and PERFORMANCE

Recent Titles in
Contributions in Political Science
Series Editor: Bernard K. Johnpoll

PROMISE and PERFORMANCE
Choosing and Implementing an Environmental Policy

ALFRED A. MARCUS

Contributions in Political Science, Number 39

GREENWOOD·PRESS
WESTPORT, CONNECTICUT • LONDON, ENGLAND

LIBRARY
The University of Texas
At San Antonio

Library of Congress Cataloging in Publication Data

Marcus, Alfred Allen, 1950-
   Promise and performance.

   (Contributions in political science; no. 39
ISSN 0147-1066)
   Bibliography: p.
   Includes index.
   1. Environmental policy—United States. 2. United
States. Environmental Protection Agency. 3. Environ-
mental law—United States. I. Title. II. Series.
HC110.E5M365   301.31'0973   79-8290
ISBN 0-313-20707-0

Library of Congress Catalog Card Number: 79-8290
ISBN: 0-313-20707-0
ISSN: 0147-1066

First published in 1980

Greenwood Press
A Division of Congressional Information Service Inc.
51 Riverside Avenue, Westport, Connecticut 06880

Printed in the United States of America

10 9 8 7 6 5 4 3 2 1

To Judy
for her sensitivity, wisdom, and understanding

Contents

Tables

Preface

Ironically, more new regulatory agencies were created while Richard Nixon was president than in any period in American history. Between 1970 and 1973, seven new agencies were created—Environmental Protection Agency (1970), National Highway Traffic Safety Administration (1970), Occupational Safety and Health Administration (1971), Consumer Product Safety Commission (1972), Mining Enforcement and Safety Administration (1973), Nuclear Regulatory Commission (1973), and Federal Energy Administration (1973). In comparison, between 1931 and 1938, the second most active period in terms of regulatory growth, only six new agencies came into being—Food and Drug Administration (1930), Securities and Exchange Commission (1934), Federal Communications Commission (1934), National Labor Relations Board (1935), Federal Maritime Commission (1936), and Civil Aeronautics Board (1938).[1] The agencies created in the more recent period have been called "new social" regulatory agencies to distinguish them from the earlier regulatory agencies which primarily controlled the economic affairs of business.[2] The new agencies were designed to control the internal production processes of industries, their relations with employees, and the features of the products they make— not just price, entry, and industry structure, the concerns of most of the older regulatory agencies.

A growing uneasiness about the effectiveness of government extends to these new regulatory agencies. Many Americans believe that the liberal social reforms of the 1960s were misconceived and misdirected, for example, that the War on Poverty led to community conflict or that the movement to end racial discrimination led to reverse discrimination.[3]

Liberalism—as an ideology of government intervention and planned social change—is in jeopardy.[4] Although most Americans continue to believe that the government should play an active role in trying to solve social problems, few still have confidence in the ability of the state to achieve what it sets out to do.[5]

A concern about the crisis of liberalism, about the gap that people perceive between what the government promises and what it performs, influenced the writing of this book. It deals with one of the new regulatory programs created in the early 1970s—the Environmental Protection Agency (EPA). It discusses its origins and early development from 1970 when the agency was created to 1977 when its major air and water pollution control laws were amended. This book stresses choices made in the period immediately before EPA actually came into existence and traces later developments insofar as they relate to these earlier choices. By looking at subsequent policy developments in terms of the agency's initial commitments, it compares the promise of the EPA with its performance.

This book had its origins in a consulting report that I wrote for the National Academy of Sciences (NAS). In June 1973, the Subcommittee on Agriculture, Environmental, and Consumer Protection of the Appropriations Committee of the House of Representatives began extensive hearings on the activities of EPA. In the ensuing appropriations bill for fiscal year 1974, EPA was directed to provide $5 million to the academy for advisory studies of the agency. Under NAS direction, study committees to address four areas of inquiry were established. The Committee on Environmental Decision-Making (CEDM) was one of these.

From December 1975 to August 1976 I served as a consultant to the Panel on Organizational and Social Considerations of the Committee on Environmental Decision-Making. Members of this committee discerned a gap between ideals and reality in the choosing and implementing of environmental policies. They took heed of Machiavelli's famous dictim: "There is such a gap between how we live and how we should live that he who neglects what is done for what should be done will learn how to accomplish his ruin, not his preservation." I was enlisted by the committee to write an "analytic history of the EPA" that would describe actual decision-making and suggest reasons for the nonattainment of ideals.

When I started my investigations, the debates between environmentalists and industrialists—between those who issued dire warnings about continued rapid industrial growth and those who maintained that continued expansion was necessary for national prosperity—were raging.[6] Concerned that the quest for environmental quality go to extremes and limit economic opportunity but equally concerned about the natural and physical limits to continued growth, my view was neither that of a committed environmentalist nor that of an ardent opponent of environmental causes.

I was interested in government regulation of business because of its alleged failings and perversities. The regulatory agencies commonly described in the academic literature performed inadequately. They were "captured" by the businesses they were supposed to regulate, had a will of their own, pursued their own suvival needs without regard for the public interest, or had some other failing.[7]

How had environmental policy been chosen and implemented? My study took four steps. First, I established initial contact with EPA officials and obtained copies of documents and other available books and articles on the agency's origin and development. Second, I gained access to the John F. Kennedy School of Government case study files. Since its inception, the Kennedy School, like Harvard Business School, has had a program that prepares case studies for classroom instructional purposes. However, unlike Harvard Business School, the Kennedy School case study program is fairly recent. Many of the earliest cases have to do with EPA's birth, development, and the decisions it made in the first years of its existence.[8] My reading of the Kennedy School case study documents was an invaluable aid in carrying out the next stage of my research.

The next stage involved spending time in Washington conducting interviews. I used participant-observer and clinical methods to gather fresh data and gain new insights.

Between February and June 1976 I interviewed 106 present and former EPA officials. I also talked to assorted Commerce Department officials, journalists, private attorneys, and staff members from various congressional committees. In exchange for a frank discussion of the issues I promised my respondents full anonymity. I tried to elicit from them comments about the following topics:

1. *The respondent's role in EPA activities and decision-making.* What role did he or she play in EPA activities and decisions? What was the nature of his or her job, how did he or she carry it out, and how did his or her work affect, if at all, agency decision-making?

2. *The history of the agency and the respondent's role in agency history.* What was the respondent's knowledge of agency history? Was he or she a relative newcomer or had the respondent worked for one of the predecessor bureaus and offices? What was his or her professional credentials, background, and training? What brought the respondent to EPA and why was he or she working in the field of environmental protection?

3. *The influence of external constraints on decision-making.* In the opinion of the respondent, what influence did the agency's statutes, Congress, the White House, other federal agencies and departments, state and local officials, private firms and groups, citizen organizations, recent events, and public opinion have on decision-making?

4. *The influence of internal constraints on decision-making.* What impact did the fact that EPA was composed of programs from other federal agencies, each presumably with its own staff and philosophy, have on decision-making? What was the impact of rivalries between offices? What was the impact of diverse professional perspectives?

5. *Deviations from ideals and suggestions for improvements.* How did EPA deviate from decision-making ideals? How could its decision-making be improved?

Insofar as possible I tried to become "socialized" into the

system of which my respondents were a part—to learn how they thought, perceived, and evaluated.[9]

The fourth stage in my research involved reading documents given to me by my respondents. Of particular importance in this regard (in that it formed the basis for one of the chapters of this book) were the files of the staff group that helped to design EPA. When I returned to Cambridge and assembled the material I had collected, my office—with various EPA documents scattered about—began to resemble a collage of the offices of the officials I had recently visited.

The report I wrote for the National Academy of Sciences was entitled "The Limitations of Comprehensive Environmental Management." One of its recommendations (included in the summary volume of the studies on EPA that NAS prepared) was that Congress had to alter the statutory framework within which EPA operated.[10] Existing laws did not adequately take into account interconnections among different forms of pollution, and fragmentation often resulted in inefficient, confusing, and counterproductive regulatory decisions.

I also wrote my dissertation (in government at Harvard under James Q. Wilson and Arthur Maas) on the basis of research I did for the academy, and I composed a chapter for a book on the politics of regulation (edited by Professor Wilson) that is based on this research, but I was concerned that in none of these studies—the NAS report, the dissertation, or the chapter—had I addressed adequately the questions that motivated my original inquiry. How was environmental policy created and carried out? Were there decision-making or implementation ideals that EPA should have attained, but was not achieving? This book, which is an effort to synthesize my writing and thinking in this area, returns to these original questions.

A Note on Methodology

It has been argued that descriptive research of the kind I have undertaken is only a "jumping-off point" for the development of "true" social science.[11] Freud's case histories, for example, are supposed to have laid the foundation for modern "scientific" psychology. Freud himself argued that case studies are only the "beginning of scientific activity," and many social scientists regard descriptive case research as an "early stage" in scientific discovery. However, there is no solid evidence that such an evolutionary view of social science uniformly applies. Most descriptive studies do not become the basis for further research, but stand alone on the basis of their merit and the interest of their subject matter.

I offer this study of EPA with two purposes in mind. First, I think it has intrinsic merit as a descriptive study. It provides important information and analysis. Second, I hope that it can help clarify and refine some of the initial efforts at model building in a relatively new area of social science, the study of policy choice and policy implementation. What this new field is and how my work may contribute to it will be more fully explored in the introduction that follows.

Notes

1. See "Government Intervention," *Business Week* (April 4, 1977), pp. 52-56.

2. William Lilley, III, and James C. Miller, III, "The New 'Social Regulation,' " *The Public Interest* (Spring 1977), pp. 49-62.

3. See Daniel P. Moynihan, *Maximum Feasible Misunderstanding* (New York: The Free Press, 1970); and Nathan Glazer, *Affirmative Discrimination: Ethnic Inequality and Public Policy* (New York: Basic Books, Inc., 1975).

4. Thomas R. Dye, *Understanding Public Policy*, 3rd ed. (Englewood Cliffs, N. J.: Prentice-Hall, 1978), p. 6.

5. Daniel Yankelovich, "On the Legitimacy of Business," *Issues in Business and Society*, George A. Steiner and John F. Steiner, 2nd ed. (New York: Random House, 1977), pp. 76-80.

6. See for instance Mancur Olson and Hans H. Landsberg, eds., *The No-Growth Society* (New York: W. W. Norton, 1973).

7. See for instance Marver H. Bernstein, *Regulating Business by Independent Commission* (Princeton, N. J.: Princeton University Press, 1955) for a statement of the "capture" theory. Louis Jaffee and Paul MacAvoy have argued that agencies are not so much industry-oriented or consumer-oriented as regulation-oriented. They are in "the regulation business" and

regulate they will, with or without a rationale. For a summary of the MacAvoy and Jaffee argument, as well as some additional arguments of his own, see James Q. Wilson, "The Dead Hand of Regulation," *The Public Interest* (Fall 1971).

8. See C. J. Christenson and G. B. Mills, "Design for Environmental Protection" (1975); J. L. Bower, "William D. Ruckelshaus and the Environmental Protection Agency" (1975); P. B. Heymann, "Senator Muskie and the 1970 Amendments to the Clean Air Act" (1978); and P. B. Heymann, "Senator Muskie and the 1970 Amendments to the Clean Air Act: Epilogue" (1978)—all at Cambridge, Mass.: John F. Kennedy School of Government.

9. See Paul Diesing, *Patterns of Discovery in the Social Sciences* (Chicago: Aldine Atherton, 1971).

10. National Research Council, *Perspectives on Technical Information for Environmental Protection*, Vol. 1 (Washington, D. C.: National Academy of Sciences, 1977).

11. See Julian L. Simon, *Basic Research Methods in Social Science: The Art of Empirical Investigation*, 2nd ed. (New York: Random House, 1978), p. 45.

Acknowledgments

It is commonplace to say that a book would not have been possible without the encouragement and support of many individuals, and in this instance the cliché is true and needs to be repeated. I especially would like to thank John Steinbruner for evaluating and criticizing the work I did for the National Academy of Sciences; Larry McCray for facilitating the research I did in Washington and for being receptive to my ideas; and J. Clarence Davies for reading the reports that I wrote for the academy and parts of this book when it was in earlier form. I also benefited from discussions I had with Robert Burt, Nathan Karch, Raphael Kasper, Richard Lowerre, Steven Lieberman, Marian Jellinek, and Stanley Bach, all of whom worked on various aspects of the studies that the academy did for the Environmental Protection Agency.

I also owe a debt of gratitude to the John F. Kennedy School of Government case study program and to Stephanie Gould, who introduced me to the EPA material prepared by the school. My students at Harvard explored the literature on government regulation and pollution control with me and provided helpful insights.

Finally, this book would have been impossible without the support and encouragement of James Q. Wilson. If there is any excellence to be found in this work, it owes its existence to Professor Wilson's efforts.

PROMISE and PERFORMANCE

Introduction: Policy Choice and Policy Implementation

This book is about the choosing and implementing of an environmental policy. Policy is what governments choose to do. Implementation is what they actually do. What governments promise when they create a policy is not identical to what they perform when they carry out a policy. A decision made at a particular moment to accomplish a goal does not mean that the decision will be carried out or that the goal will be accomplished.

In recent years the focus of political science has shifted from a traditional concern with institutions, processes, and behavior to a new concern with public policy. Policy analysis has been defined as the effort to explain the causes and consequences of policy.[1] Sometimes analysts view policy as a "dependent variable" and try to determine how social and political factors influence the choice of policy. In other studies, they view policy as an "independent variable" and try to discover what effect policy has had on society and politics. This book combines these approaches.

Analyzing the causes and consequences of policy is not the same as advocating changes in policy. Although analysis may be a precondition of advocacy, analysis and advocacy are separate activities. To analyze is to explore systematically and to try to understand the nature of existing policy,

while to advocate is to use "rhetoric, persuasion, organization, and activism" to change the nature of existing policy.[2]
This book is an exercise in analysis not advocacy.

Although many factors influence policy development,
"authorities"—executives, legislators, and administrators—
actually choose and implement policy.[3] They enact legislation, issue reorganization orders, and take administrative
actions that give expression to the goals, direction, and content of government action. This book is about these "authorities"-the White House, Congress, and the bureaucracy and
how they chose and implemented an environmental policy.

The first part deals with the process of policy choice. In
1970 the White House issued a reorganization order that
brought together programs from three departments and
created the Environmental Protection Agency. In the same
year Congress passed a new Clean Air Act that committed
the agency to achieving specific goals by certain dates.
Chapter 1 traces the process of formulating the reorganization order; Chapter 2, the process of drafting the 1970 Clean
Air Act.

While the first part of this book is about policy choice, the
second part is about policy implementation. Implementation
refers to actions taken to achieve objectives set forth in prior
policy decisions.[4] It involves the carrying out of authoritative policy decisions by the bureaucracy. Before the bureaucracy can implement policy, its members must perceive what
it is they are supposed to do. The process of implementation
involves a stage of receiving instructions that is prior to the
stage of actually carrying out these instructions. Chapters 3
and 4 are about the reception of policy instructions. Their
focus is the new administrator and the civil servants that
EPA inherited and how they received the instructions that
the White House and Congress meant to convey. Chapters 5
and 6 discuss the second stage of policy implementation—
the actual carrying out of policy once instructions are
received. Chapter 5 covers the enforcement of the 1970 Clean
Air Act, while Chapter 6 covers the enforcement of the 1972
Federal Water Pollution Control Act. By examining in Part I
the process of policy choice and in Part II, the movement of

policy instructions through the two stages of implementation, this book compares EPA's promise with its performance.

Government Performance

Americans are increasingly concerned about the performance of government. The Great Society was a historical period in the Johnson administration when commitment to achieving rapid social progress through government action was at its peak. Legislation that had been awaiting adoption for years was enacted, and new programs and new agencies were created in unprecedented numbers. The unprecedented growth of agencies and programs continued into the middle years of the Nixon administration, when between 1970 and 1973 more new regulatory agencies were created than in any other period in American history.

By the early 1970s, however, Americans were increasingly skeptical about government claims and accomplishments. After the well-publicized failures of many social programs and events, such as the war in Vietnam and the Watergate break-in and subsequent revelations, faith in governmental action as a source of social improvement was badly shaken. Many people doubted whether bureaucracies were effective, and many believed they were beyond the control of the people and their elected officials.

How can the performance of a government bureaucracy be evaluated? Criteria cannot be established scientifically. Standards are affected by the values, perceptions, and interests of the institutions and individuals who do the evaluation. James Q. Wilson has formulated two "laws" to cover research that purports to evaluate program performance.

Wilson's First Law: All policy interventions in social problems produce the intended effect—if the research is carried out by those implementing the policy or their friends.

Wilson's Second Law: No policy intervention in social problems produces the intended effect—if the research is carried out by independent third parties, especially those skeptical of the policy.[5]

Policy evaluation is a social process.[6] What is viewed as "correct," "effective," "corrupt," or "responsive" depends on the position and circumstance of the institutions and individuals that assess performance.[7]

Judgments made by policymakers and administrators about the worth of particular programs, often are impressionistic, based upon anecdotal and fragmentary evidence, and strongly influenced by ideology, self-interest, and other personal criteria.[8] Much conflict comes about because of the subjective nature of evaluation. Evaluators, using different criteria, reach different conclusions about the merits of the same program.

Efforts to overcome the subjective nature of evaluation have led to the development of various "objective" indicators of program performance. For example, Robert Backoff suggests eighteen separate criteria that can be used for evaluating bureaucratic performance: seven that measure subunit operational performance, three that measure overall organization effectiveness, two that refer to the organization's freedom of action, and six that measure societal impact.[9] An advantage of using criteria, such as those suggested by Backoff, is the ability to make comparisons between programs. For example, all programs could be compared with respect to efficiency, organizational effectiveness, or contribution to social welfare. However, there is no empirical evidence that demonstrates that Backoff's categories are or can be used in evaluating actual government programs. Backoff makes no effort to demonstrate that government actors would actually use his categories, especially in the systematic and comprehensive way he suggests.

Wilson derives his criteria from the perceptions of groups involved in the policy process.[10] He argues that the president and his staff favor accountability; lawyers and the courts stress equity; business leaders and economists emphasize efficiency; individual citizens and their representatives care most about responsiveness; while the "political outs who want in" are most concerned about fiscal integrity. In support of Wilson's method, Peter Winch in *The Idea of a Social*

TABLE 1
Backoff's Criteria for Evaluating
Program Performance*

A. Subunit Operational Performance

1. Efficiency—the ratio of input to output.
2. Production—the number of output units produced in a time period.
3. Productivity—the rate of increase in production in a specified time period.
4. Production quality—the qualitative change in the output units over time.
5. Production effectiveness—the extent to which the subunit goals relative to a stipulated time period are achieved.
6. Product or service innovation—the number of new products or services produced by the subunit relative to a time period of assessment.
7. Job or work satisfaction—the degree of subunit employee satisfaction with the work in the organization.

B. Overall Organizational Effectiveness

1. Organization effectiveness—the degree of goal achievement for the organization.
2. Organization innovation—the degree to which properties of the bureaucracy are changed in a particular time.
3. Organization morale—the degree of employee satisfaction and identification with organization.

C. Organizational Freedom of Action

1. Organization power over task elements—the extent to which the bureaucracy has the capacity to satisfy needs of its task environment.
2. Organizational dependence on task elements—the extent to which the bureaucracy depends on its task environment to satisfy needs.

D. Societal Impact Performance

1. Representativeness—the degree to which values, norms,

*Adapted from Robert Backoff, "Operationalizing Administrative Reform for Improved Governmental Performance," *Administration and Society* (May, 1974), pp. 96-99.

and personnel characteristics are congruent with those in the wider society.

2. Responsiveness—the extent to which the bureaucracy is open to satisfying the needs of the citizenry in the amount of time required to do so.

3. Accountability—the extent to which the bureaucracy is subject to monitoring and control from environmental units (legislative, judicial, press, etc.).

4. Persuasiveness—the extent to which the bureaucracy avoids coercive means and the extent to which it relies on persuasive influence in attaining its goals and attending to client relations.

5. Effectiveness—the extent to which the bureaucracy fulfills the goals of the society.

6. Social welfare—the extent to which the bureaucracy contributes to the net social welfare of the society as a result of its activities (net of costs and benefits).

Science argues that the criteria for judging social action should not be those of the observer, but those of the observed.[11] If evaluative criteria are imposed from the outside, they may not be appropriate to the actual situation, i.e., to the constraints and opportunities the White House and Congress imposed on the bureaucracy and to the circumstances under which the program was actually carried out. However, how do we know that Wilson's criteria are the ones the White House and Congress actually applied? In this instance, did the president and his staff favor accountability, and individual citizens and their congressmen care most about responsiveness?

This book will argue that the White House and Congress had different criteria for assessing EPA performance, but the basic differences in what the two branches were seeking were not accountability and responsiveness. The White House had a broad policy orientation and was seeking what Backoff terms social welfare and efficiency (note D.6 and A.1 in Table 1), while Congress had a narrower program orientation and was seeking what Backoff calls organizational and

TABLE 2
Wilson's Criteria for Evaluating Program Performance *

---

1. Accountability or control—getting the bureaucracy to accomplish agreed-upon national goals.
2. Equity—treating like cases alike on the basis of clear rules known in advance.
3. Efficiency—maximizing output for a given level of expenditure or minimizing expenditure for a given output.
4. Responsiveness—inducing bureaucrats to meet with alacrity and compassion cases that cannot be brought under single rational rules.
5. Fiscal integrity—properly spending and accounting for public money.

*Adapted from James Q. Wilson, "The Bureaucracy Problem," *The Public Interest* (Winter, 1967), pp. 3-9.

---

production effectiveness (note B.1 and A.5 in Table 1). The White House evaluated EPA in terms of its ability to achieve progress in environmental protection at the least total expense to society. Congress, on the other hand, evaluated the agency in terms of its ability to achieve intended results by certain dates regardless of the total costs to society.

Congress had a program orientation, while the White House had a policy orientation. Daniel P. Moynihan makes this distinction between the concepts: "Programs are related to a single part of the system; policy seeks to respond to the system in its entirety."[12] From the White House, EPA received orders to deal with the environment in a comprehensive manner. The reorganization order issued by the president at the time of the agency's birth called for the elimination of artificial distinctions between pollution control programs. It advocated perceiving the environment as a totality, tracing the flow of contaminants through the ecosystem, and making the least costly pollution reduction decisions. Meanwhile, Congress continued to pass separate air, water, and solid waste pollution statutes that made the holistic approach the White House advocated difficult, if not impossible, to carry out.

There were elements in the White House, such as the Council on Environmental Quality (CEQ), with a genuine desire to see rapid progress in a short time period, but there were competing elements, the Council of Economic Advisers (CEA) and the Office of Management and Budget (OMB) that advocated achievements over a longer duration and had more influence on the president. In addition, there was the broad national constituency that the White House represented. Representing this constituency meant that the White House could not afford to ignore the net costs and benefits of EPA decisions.

Individual congressmen, on the other hand, represented narrower and less diverse constituencies.[13] Policy in Congress was generally determined by powerful committee chairmen, such as Senator Edmund Muskie (D.—Maine), who had a special reputational and career interest in air and water pollution issues. In such areas as pollution control, Muskie, other congressmen, and the committees they headed were the dominant forces. There was no centralized leadership in Congress to integrate diverse perspectives, no commanding figure—such as a head of state—to resolve competing priorities. Congress, in contrast to the White House, was more able to stress specific pollution control programs within a limited time frame and to ignore the broader implications of environmental decisions—the possible "spillovers" and unintended consequences of making rapid progress in a short period of time.

WHAT WAS ACHIEVED

In assessing government performance, policy analysts make a distinction between outputs and outcomes.[14] Outputs are what the government does (building bridges, spending money, issuing regulations). Outcomes, on the other hand, are the ultimate impacts of government action—the long-term effects on social, political, and economic conditions: the bridges that government builds may promote the economic growth and prosperity of a region; the money it spends may prevent the impoverishment of people who otherwise could not earn a living; the regulations it issues may increase the average life span of citizens over the long term. Ideally, evaluations of government performance should be concerned with outcomes, but outcomes are harder to measure. It is easy enough to measure direct costs in terms of resources devoted to a program, for example, but more difficult to measure indirect costs including the opportunities lost to do other things. There is the problem of computing short-term benefits compared to long-term benefits, the problem of comparing tangible costs and benefits with intangible costs and benefits, and the problem of measuring differential impacts on classes and groups of people.[15] Measurement is confounded by the existence of unintended consequences. Sometimes the more important impacts of a program are not those that directly affect target situations and groups but those that affect situations and groups other than those that have been targeted.

For all these reasons implementation analysts generally concentrate on outputs that can be observed and measured.[16] This book assesses performance in terms of outputs—whether or not a decision-making procedure to calculate societal costs and benefits was used; an organizational design to achieve comprehensive management was put into place; administrative deadlines to make program progress were met; and explicit standards of program effectiveness achieved. I argue that EPA was responsive to the wishes of Congress and the White House. Chapter 3 will show that the first administrator, William Ruckelshaus, sought to adhere faithfully to the timetables mandated by Congress, but he also inaugurated a decision-making procedure that involved analysis of regulatory costs and benefits. Chapter 4 will show that the two branches also influenced the organizational form and internal structure of the new environmental agency. EPA was partially organized to approach pollution control problems from the broad, comprehensive perspective that the White House advocated, and it was partially organized to carry out the specific programmatic activities that Congress mandated. EPA responded to the wishes of the two branches but pleased neither branch completely.

EPA was part-servant to the White House and part-servant to Congress even when the demands of the two branches conflicted. Chapter 5 on air pollution enforcement will show that a presidential initiative, the president's 1974 energy policy, contradicted congressional intentions. It called for the increased use of coal and delayed the achievement of the 1975 healthy air goal established by Congress. Chapter 6 on water pollution enforcement, on the other hand, will show that a congressional initiative, the passage of the 1972 Federal Water Pollution Control Act in spite of a presidential veto, blocked the realization of executive ambitions. This new act burdened the bureaucracy with an additional regulatory burden that left it without the time it needed to do the economic analysis that the White House was seeking. As the agent of two branches with conflicting demands EPA achieved some progress in cleaning the air and removing contaminants from the water, and it took some precautions to assess the economic consequences and the energy implications of its actions, but it did not satisfy either branch entirely.

Problems in Policy Choice and Policy Implementation

In recent years the scholarly literature on program performance has grown rapidly. In general the literature has been pessimistic about the prospects for planned social change. The message has been that governments create expectations they cannot fulfill, that they make promises they cannot carry out.

Why do programs fail to achieve goals established by the White House and Congress? Many reasons have been cited: overly ambitious goals; goals too general in nature to be operationalized; the lack of available technology to achieve goals; and changing social and political circumstances that lead to the abandonment of goals once they have been established.[17] Much of the scholarly literature has focused on problems in policy choice and implementation. Previously, scholars focused on the former problems.[18] Recently, scholars have paid more attention to the latter. Implementation studies assume that a policy already has been chosen. According to Paul Berman

Implementation analysis is *not* about whether a policy's goals are fit and proper, which is a matter of values; nor does it concern itself with how they were chosen, which is a study of policy-making.... Implementation analysis is ... the study of why authoritative decisions [policies, plans, laws] do not lead to expected results. To speak in more positive terms, it is the study of conditions under which authoritative decisions do lead to desired outcomes.[19]

Berman, at least, admits that implementation analysis is not only about the conditions under which policies fail. Unlike the study of policy choices, he argues that the analysis of implementation focuses on results. It examines intentions only insofar as they are relevant to outcomes.

Like the scholars of policy choice, the scholars of policy implementation generally have created ideal models of rational behavior and compared these ideal models with the way policy is actually chosen and implemented. The scholars of policy implementation have done so less explicitly than the scholars of policy choice, but implicit in the work of both policy choice and implementation analysts are models from classical economic and organization theories that describe the behavior of the goal-maximizing rational decision maker and the goal-maximizing rational organization.

The goal-maximizing organization would act in the following manner. It would: (1) identify a problem and its causes; (2) clarify and rank goals; (3) collect all relevant options for meeting the problem and all available information on the options; (4) predict the consequences of each option and assess to what extent it would achieve desired outcomes; and (5) select the alternative that came closest to maximizing goal achievement.[20] The goal-maximizing organization would then implement the option chosen by rational decision making methods. It would: (1) receive without distortion or confusion the instructions given by a single decision maker; (2) adhere closely to these instructions, deviating from them only to improve performance; and (3) attempt to maximize intended outcomes and minimize unintended outcomes within a specified period of time.

Of course, this description of decision-making and organizational performance is an idealization of machine-like calculation and compliance. In actual practice it is seldom realized. Scholars have pointed out that actual policy choice suffers from analytic and political limitations and that actual implementation suffers from problems, such as the exercise of discretionary authority and the complexity of joint action.

ANALYTIC AND POLITICAL LIMITATIONS

The analytic limitations to rational policy choice include constraints on attempts to obtain information necessary for calculating maximal goals, and the tendency to find a course of action that will satisfy minimal goals, which is known as "satisficing" rather than maximizing. Actual decision makers have neither the time nor the information to carry out all the steps in the rational decision-making process. Human intellectual capacities are limited and analysis is expensive. In actual cases, the analysis that is done is drastically limited. Problems are not defined carefully, goals are not clarified, important alternatives are neglected, and important outcomes cannot be anticipated. According to John Steinbruner, decisions are made on the basis of incomplete information,[21] simplistic decision rules, and a cognitive inability to recognize and assimilate dissonant information.

Policies are not adopted because they are the most appropriate from an analytic perspective but because policymakers agree and are willing to accept them. To obtain agreement and to make a policy acceptable is a political process.

Political ambitions play a role, as do competing interests. "The maneuvers whereby political actors seek to convince, bargain with, cajole, and coerce each other" are inherent features of the way policy is actually chosen.[22] To reach agreement, negotiation, compromise, and mutual adjustment are necessary. The famous bureaucratic-politics paradigm of Graham Allison explicitly portrays decision-making as a political process.[23] According to Allison, decisions are not derived by "detached analysts focusing coolly *on* the problem."[24] "Players" with parochial priorities, interests, and stakes share in the making of decisions. Policy is a "political outcome," the endpoint of political maneuvers by interested political and bureaucratic players.

Criticism of Environmental Policy

Most of the scholarly criticism of environmental policy focuses on the problems of policy choice. Charles O. Jones discusses a process that affected the passage of the 1970 Clean Air Act that he calls "speculative augmentation." He writes that in 1970

Public demonstrations and opinion polls projected a clear message to decision-makers: "Do something dramatic about pollution." Denied the process of moderating policy choices in light of existing knowledge and capabilities, policy-makers were left to speculate as intelligently as they could, both about what would satisfy the public and whether the policy devised could in fact be enforced.[25]

Jones suggests that policymakers did not "speculate" wisely. The air pollution policy chosen was geared toward pleasing an aroused public. It was guided by inadequate information and analysis and tended to be extreme, blind, and unpredictable.

James Q. Wilson has a similar view. To obtain passage of the 1970 Clean Air Act, it was necessary to get congressmen "to take the problem seriously, to forge a winning coalition among [them]...and to overcome the arguments and influence of opponents."[26] Accomplishing this in a "representative government," Wilson maintains requires the recitation of powerful arguments, the evocation of horror stories, or the mobilization of a broad political movement. Political inertia is not easily overcome, and when it is overcome, it is often at the price of exaggerating the virtue of those who are to benefit...or the wickedness of those who bear the burden...[27]

Wilson suggests that policy, chosen in a nonideal fashion, was deficient. He cites work done by Henry Jacoby and John Steinbruner on the 1970 Clean Air Act.[28] This act required auto manufacturers to reduce hydrocarbon and carbon monoxide emissions by 90 percent by 1975 and nitrous oxide emissions by the same amount one year later. The chief difficulty with these standards, which were imposed in a short period of time, was that they required the auto manufacturers to commit themselves to improving the existing technology—the internal combustion engine. The 1975 deadline gave the manufacturers no incentive to search for a more promising alternative, such as a steam engine, gas turbine, or electric motor, to the standard internal combustion engine.

Jones points out that the air pollution policy, chosen in less than ideal fashion, was likely to be implemented in a nonideal way. He applies a "life cycle" theory to the process of implementation. According to this theory, agencies rapidly pass through stages that lead them from the vigor of their "youth" to the debilitation of "old age."[29] After jubilant beginnings with high expectations and massive political support, they decline and perform inadequately when the original public that supported passage of their legislation loses interest.

Jones and Wilson, political scientists interested in the politics of legislative decision-making and the impact of policy choice on implementation, are not alone in criticizing existing environmental policy. Although scientists and engineers have also criticized this policy,[30] it is economists who stand out as the major critics of existing environmental policy.[31] Many of them argue that relying upon the dictates of the government to set standards is too costly and administratively burdensome. Instead of relying upon direct government regulation, they propose that some form of incentive system be used. They have devised various incentive schemes-pollution taxes, effluent charges, and "auctions" for pollution rights. The advantage of using these schemes is that they take the burden of choice from central governmental decision makers who generally lack sufficient knowledge of specific industrial conditions to make optimal decisions. They reduce the coercive power of the state and restore market-like decision-making, thereby both decreasing the total cost to society and minimizing administrative complexity.

Economists generally believe that from an analytical perspective incentive systems have many advantages particularly when they are compared to direct regulation. Why haven't these schemes been used? Although there are technical reasons for their nonadoption, opposition also has come from environmentalists, fearful that the adoption of incentives would signify the granting to industry of "licenses to pollute"; from industrialists, worried that the price of pollution would be set "too high"; from Treasury Department officials not willing to use pollution charges as a means of revenue collection; and from legislators, such as Senator Muskie, who have been committed to the present scheme of direct regulation.[32] This opposition has made their adoption politically unfeasible.

One dissenting voice opposed to the general criticism of existing policy is Helen Ingram.[33] She admits that the policy established in 1970 set "bold goals" that reached "well beyond" what could be attained; yet she defends the policy of setting "bold goals" and maintains that it was rational, not from the perspective of the rules of classical decision-making, but from the perspective of "political decision-making." What she means by this rationality is that "under certain circumstances, postulating a symbolically appealing goal that goes substantially beyond what has been achieved in the past is preferable to endorsing more limited ambitions."[34] She maintains that from the perspective of the "political activist" the environmental policy chosen in 1970 was rational. For the political activist rationality means "seizing favorable opportunities."[35] "An activist," Ingram argues, "must... be watchful of opportunities to exercise influence."[36] If mistakes are made because of the activist's opportunism, she contends that these mistakes can be corrected sometime in the future. She writes that it is rational "to shift the burden" for the correction of "innovative policies" to future policymakers who "ipso facto" will be "more experienced."[37]

How This Account Differs

Ingram, Wilson, and Jones discuss the passage of new environmental legislation from the perspective of congressional policymaking, but policymaking was not by congressional enactment alone. An adequate investigation cannot fail to disregard the crucial role played by the White House in choosing and carrying out an environmental policy. It cannot fail to ignore the circumstances under which a new agency for environmental protection was brought into being. This account, therefore, differs from earlier versions in that it focuses both on the creation of EPA and on the passage of new pollution control legislation.

While environmental policy was not chosen rationally, it was innovative. Ingram has to redefine rationality to defend environmental policymaking. Her new definition of rationality is that of the "political activist." While policy may have been rational from this perspective, it was not rational from the perspective of the rules of classic decision making theory.

This account will show that in choosing policy the White House and Congress started by considering single alternatives. These alternatives were modified by a political process that involved other political actors. These actors brought up new alternatives that had not been originally considered. Decision-making involved making a proposal, modifying the proposal in response to the counterproposals and pressures of the other interested actors, and adopting what remained of the proposal after it had been modified by this political process. Although there was some consideration of consequences and weighing of outcomes, there was no systematic analysis.

The major impulse in the making of environmental policy was the thrust for rapid agreement, the impulse to make a proposal and to accept it as rapidly as possible. The year 1970 was an extraordinary one with respect to the opportunity to make environmental policy. Prior to 1967, few people recognized the importance of the pollution control issue, but after 1967, public awareness grew rapidly. In 1970, public opinion polls showed that pollution control, next to crime, was the nation's leading priority.[38] Millions of Americans took part in demonstrations to bring to the public's awareness the harmful effects of pollution. Politicians in and out of the White House championed environmental causes, and media attention focused on these causes. A broad constituency, willing to support almost any proposal offered by the politicians, existed. This constituency consisted of young and old, businessmen and union representatives, environmentalists and industrialists, scientific experts and lay persons, and establishment figures and protest leaders. Almost everyone who at the time commanded political attention or clout was anxious to see a new policy adopted.

This atmosphere contributed to hasty decision-making; and the precipitious action taken in response to the aroused national constituency did not involve careful problem definition, extended examination of outcomes, or comparison of alternatives. Direct regulation, for instance, was chosen without consideration of incentives.

The policy formulated was not chosen rationally, if rationality is defined by the rules of classic decision-making, but it was innovative in a way that Ingram does not consider. Ingram understands innovation to be large-scale conceptual change. The "concept" of clean air she writes

changed significantly through the legislative process in 1970. The pragmatic, functional definition of air quality, restricted to what was economically and technologically feasible, was abandoned, and clean air was legislated a fundamental national value.[39]

This book, however, holds that innovation in the case of environmental policy was not restricted to the conceptual change that Ingram mentions.

The policy established in 1970 was innovative in that it made use of two of the most widely celebrated and universally endorsed proposals for regulatory reform. First, it established the principal of executive integration. Successful regulation, it has been argued by many political scientists, legal scholars, and public administration specialists, can only occur when the White House becomes more directly involved in the regulatory process.[40] Regulatory agencies should be more directly accountable to the White House. To increase White House influence, the pollution control responsibilities of EPA were not combined with other natural resource responsibilities as some had suggested. What became EPA was not buried in the bottom of a new Department of Natural Resources as was proposed. Instead the new Environmental Protection Agency was given a separate pollution control mission, independent status, and an administrator chosen by the president.

Second, the agency had statutes that defined with some precision the role and the responsibility of the regulators. Since the 1950s, critics of regulatory administration have asserted that unclear legal authority is a major reason for the lack of effective enforcement. In 1954 Louis Jaffe wrote that "much of what agencies do is the expectable consequence of their broad and ill-defined power. The fault, if fault there be, is at least as much in the statutory scheme as in the administration."[41] The belief among reformers of regulation was that agencies that were asked to administer vague statutes would protect the industries they were supposed to regulate. Timid, halting, and uncreative regulatory policies would be the result. EPA, therefore, was delegated statutes (the 1970 Clean Air Act and the 1972 Federal Water Pollution Control Act) with explicit goals, timetables, and methods for achieving goals.

In the first instance, the hope was that EPA would not have to endure plural leadership under commissioners who were more directly tied to congressional committees and special interests than they were to national policy and the White House. In the second instance, the hope was that the agency would not have to suffer doubt and confusion about what it was supposed to do and therefore succumb to the pressures of powerful interests that would dictate what it actually carried out.

By 1970, officials in the White House and Congress were sensitive to complaints that government programs failed more often than they succeeded. After the inadequate performance of various domestic and international programs in the 1960s, they sensed that a crisis of confidence in government performance was brewing. The White House, therefore, structured the new environmental agency to be more responsive to presidential wishes, and Congress granted it explicit authority so that it would adhere more closely to congressional intentions. The purpose was to bridge the gap between promise and performance, to reduce discretion, and to make EPA accountable to constitutionally sanctioned authorities.

IMPLEMENTATION

What went wrong? If innovations suggested for many years by policy analysts finally were adopted, why weren't they successfully carried out? The rational model of policy implementation implies an orderly process of receiving and carrying out instructions. It implies predictability of outcome—that the bureaucracy knows what it is supposed to do and that it does what it is told. Actual bureaucratic behavior, however, does not conform to these rational assumptions.

Discretion

One problem frequently mentioned in the scholarly literature is discretion.[42] Legal scholars have shown that most laws give bureaucrats substantial latitude for implementing policy decisions. Bureaucrats are delegated unclear authority and act on their own making decisions without regard to the instructions they have received from superiors. While some organizational theorists have challenged the whole legitimacy of hierarchical command systems and have lauded the exercise of discretion and labeled it "participation," political scientists generally have found that discretion is exercised to please significant external interests, that it leads to the "capture" of the bureaucracy by the interests it is supposed to control.

The problem of discretion is based on the common perception that lower level bureaucrats rarely do exactly what they are told, that in many instances they fail or are unable to carry out the instructions they receive. While policymakers are preoccupied with the way policy is expressed in legislation and reorganization orders, bureaucrats are concerned with how they can cope with the stress and the complexity of their immediate, everyday tasks. The rational model assumes that their behavior can be controlled by superiors, but it does not take into account the fact that individual bureaucrats resist hierarchical management, that they are creatures of custom and habit who oppose attempts to change their standard operating routines. According to James Q. Wilson, one of the central problems of a bureaucracy is getting front-line workers—the teacher, nurse, diplomat, police officer, or welfare worker—to do the "right thing."[43]

Richard Stewart, in an analysis of judicial review under the 1970 Clean Air Act, shows that discretion was at least partially kept in check by the courts.[44] Stewart holds that courts played a substantial role in checking the "parochial tendencies" of the agency, and when necessary, they interpreted relevant statutes "to enlarge the factors" which EPA had to consider. They intervened to preserve the principle of environmental diversity and generally upheld the principle of federalism by supporting the states in their refusal to implement drastic measures.

Marc Roberts and Susan Farrel, on the other hand, argue that state level bureaucrats exercised discretion without sufficient control.[45] Roberts and Farrel examined the operation of a representative sample of programs. What they found was that state agencies had substantial discretion in determining the reductions that were required of specific pollution sources and that the specific clean-up requirements were often the result of accords reached with the regulated industries.

This account does not have enough data on state agencies or judicial review to confirm or disprove Roberts and Farrel's theories. It understands the problem of discretion in the following way. Chapter 3 will show that EPA's first administrator, William Ruckelshaus, received competing directions from the White House and Congress. Discretion occurred as a response to conflicting instructions. When the bureaucracy received two sets of instructions, it divided into an organism with three wills—a will directed toward achieving White House instructions, a will directed toward achieving congressional instructions, and a will that acted without regard for White House or congressional commands. Chapter 4 discusses the divisions within the bureaucracy and how the conflict between White House and congressional commands influenced these divisions.

The rational model of policy implementation assumes that goals and means are communicated with clarity and consistency to the bureaucracy. It assumes that the bureaucracy is united, that it is a single organism with a single will. These assumptions, however, did not apply to the actual carrying out of environmental policy. EPA had a dual mandate. Held accountable by branches with different philosophies and approaches to pollution control and judged by standards that were not entirely compatible with each other, the agency did not carry out policy in accord with the assumptions of the rational model.

Complexity of Joint Action

When an agency confronts a situation in which there are many participants and perspectives, when numerous decisions have to be made and many attempts have to be made to secure compliance from participants whose agreement is necessary to further the progress of the program, then the probability of success decreases and the possibility of unexpected problems increases. The problem of complexity of joint action, according to Jeffrey Pressman and Aaron Wildavsky, can involve the following conditions: (1) contradictory instructions from policymakers; (2) a bureaucracy divided into competing units with opposing interests; (3) limited time; (4) tasks that involve many steps, many decisions, and many participants; and (5) a rapidly changing political environment in which there is pervasive conflict among competing interests and values. Under conditions such as these, Pressman and Wildavsky argue that "what is

TABLE 3
The Complexity of Joint Action

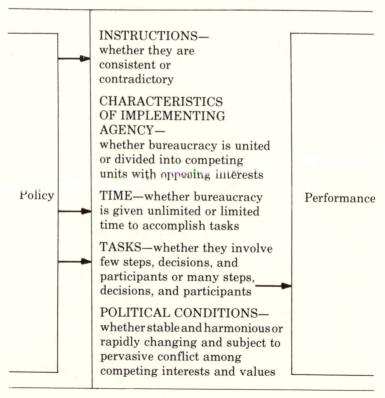

INSTRUCTIONS—
whether they are
consistent or
contradictory

CHARACTERISTICS
OF IMPLEMENTING
AGENCY—
whether bureaucracy is united
or divided into competing
units with opposing interests

Policy

TIME—whether bureaucracy
is given unlimited or limited
time to accomplish tasks

Performance

TASKS—whether they involve
few steps, decisions, and
participants or many steps,
decisions, and participants

POLITICAL CONDITIONS—
whether stable and harmonious or
rapidly changing and subject to
pervasive conflict among
competing interests and values

apparently simple and straightforward becomes complex and convoluted."[46]

This book will show that the problem of complexity first manifested itself at the instructions stage when Ruckelshaus and the bureaucracy received conflicting directions from the White House and Congress. At the carrying out of instructions stage the complexity manifested itself in the form of delay. Pressman and Wildavsky explain delay as the necessity of obtaining "simultaneous clearances" from many actors. They maintain that delay is a "function of the number of decision points, the number of participants at each point, and the intensity of their preferences."[47]

Chapters 5 and 6 demonstrate how delay affected the implementation of the 1970 Clean Air Act and the implementation of the 1972 Water Pollution Control Act. The tasks that had to be performed under these pieces of legislation involved many steps, many decisions, and many participants. The bureaucracy was given not only limited time to complete these tasks, but also had to carry them out in a rapidly changing political environment in which there was pervasive conflict among competing interests and values. Numerous approvals and clearances had to be obtained from a variety of diverse participants. In the instance of both pollution control statutes, goals were deflected, energies dissipated, and delays occurred because of the need to concert the action of numerous independent actors.[48]

EPA's ability to achieve statutory goals was limited by the existence of many actors who had to be satisfied. Accountability to many actors (White House, Congress, courts, state and local government, popular opinion) is what the constitutional system intends. A system of multiple accountability has advantages and disadvantages. One of the advantages is flexibility. The bureaucracy can bend easily and can be molded by changing circumstances. It can respond to new conditions as they develop and react to new events as they take place. One of the disadvantages is lack of predictability. A bureaucracy held in check by many forces will not achieve intended outcomes. If it does so, it will do so slowly and over a long period of time. The advantages and disadvantages of a constitutional system of multiple accountability will be discussed at greater length in the Conclusion.

Notes

1. Thomas R. Dye, *Understanding Public Policy*, 3rd ed. (Englewood Cliffs, N.J.: Prentice-Hall, 1978), p. 5.
2. Ibid., p. 7.
3. See James E. Anderson, *Public Policy-Making* (New York: Praeger, 1975), p. 3; and David Easton, *A Systems Analysis of Political Life* (New York: Wiley, 1965), p. 212.
4. C. E. Van Horn and D. S. Van Meter, "The Implementation of Intergovernmental Policy" in *Public Policy-Making in a Federal System*, ed. C. O. Jones and R. Thomas (Beverly Hills, Calif.: Sage, 1976).
5. James Q. Wilson, "On Pettigrew and Armor," *The Public Interest* (Spring 1973), pp. 132-34.
6. See David Braybrooke and Charles E. Lindblom, *A Strategy of Decision: Policy Evaluation as a Social Process*, 2nd ed. (New York: The Free Press, 1970).
7. See Robert C. Fried, *Performance in American Bureaucracy* (Boston: Little, Brown and Company, 1976).
8. Anderson, *Public Policy-Making*, p. 132.
9. Robert Backoff, "Operationalizing Administrative Reform for Improve Governmental Performance," *Administration and Society* (May 1974), pp. 96-99.
10. James Q. Wilson, "The Bureaucracy Problem," *The Public Interest* (Winter 1967), pp. 3-9.
11. Peter Winch, *The Idea of a Social Science* (New York: Humanities Press, 1958); also see John M. Johnson, *Doing Field Research* (New York: The Free Press, 1975).
12. Daniel Patrick Moynihan, "Policy vs. Program in the 1970s," *The Public Interest* (Summer 1970), reprinted in Daniel Patrick Moynihan, *Coping: Essays on the Practice of Government* (New York: The Free Press, 1971), p. 273.
13. See Lawrence C. Dodd and Bruce I. Oppenheimer, eds. *Congress Reconsidered* (New York: Praeger, 1977).
14. Anderson, *Public Policy-Making*, p. 134.
15. Dye, *Understanding Public Policy*, pp. 312-14.
16. See Aaron Wildavsky, *Speaking Truth to Power: The Art and Craft of Policy Analysis* (Boston: Little, Brown and Company, 1979), p. 355.
17. Compare with Dye, *Understanding Public Policy*, pp. 330-32 and Anderson, *Public Policy-Making*, pp. 150-53.
18. See, for example, Charles E. Lindblom, "The Science of 'Muddling Through,' " *The Public Administration Review* (Spring 1959), pp. 79-88;

Amitai Etzioni, "Mixed-Scanning: A 'Third' Approach to Decision-Making," *The Public Administration Review* (December 1967), pp. 385-92; and Irving L. Janis, *Victims of Groupthink* (Boston: Houghton Mifflin, 1972), pp. 2-13.

19. Paul Berman, "The Study of Macro-and Micro-Implementation," *Public Policy* (Spring 1978),p. 160.

20. See Anderson, *Public Policy-Making*, p. 10; Alan A. Altshuler and Norman C. Thomas, eds, *The Politics of the Federal Bureaucracy* (New York: Harper & Row, 1977), p. 113; and George C. Edwards and Ira Sharkansky, *The Policy Predicament* (San Francisco: W. H. Freeman, 1978), p. 7.

21. See John Steinbruner, *The Cybernetic Theory of Decision* (Princeton, N.J.: Princeton University Press, 1974).

22. Ibid., p. 142.

23. See Graham T. Allison, *Essence of Decision* (Boston: Little, Brown and Company, 1971).

24. Ibid., p. 175.

25. Charles O. Jones, "Speculative Augmentation in Federal Air Pollution Policy-Making," *Journal of Politics* (May 1974), pp. 438-64.

26. James Q. Wilson, "The Politics of Regulation" in *Social Responsibility and the Business Predicament*, ed. James W. McKie (Washington, D.C.: The Brookings Institution, 1974), p. 151-52.

27. Ibid.

28. Henry D. Jacoby, John D. Steinbruner, et al., *Clearing the Air: Federal Policy on Automotive Emissions Control* (Cambridge, Mass.: Ballinger, 1973).

29. Marver Bernstein, *Regulating Business by Independent Commission* (Princeton, N. J.: Princeton University Press, 1955).

30. Helen Ingram, "The Political Rationality of Innovation: The Clean Air Act Amendments of 1970" in *Approaches to Controlling Air Pollution*, ed. Ann F. Friedlaender (Cambridge, Mass.: MIT Press, 1978), p. 12.

31. Environment and National Resources Policy Division, Congressional Research Service, Library of Congress, *Pollution Taxes, Effluent Charges and Other Alternatives for Pollution Control* (Washington, D.C.: U. S. Government Printing Office, 1977).

32. James E. Anderson, David W. Brady, and Charles Bullock, III, *Public Policy and Politics in America* (North Scituate, Mass.: Duxbury Press, 1978), p. 89.

33. Ingram, "Political Rationality."

34. Ibid., p. 13.

35. Ibid., p. 14.

36. Ibid.

37. Ibid., p. 13.

38. See J. Clarence Davies, III, and Barbara S. Davies, *The Politics of Pollution*, 2nd ed. (Indianapolis: Bobbs-Merrill, 1975), pp. 80-86.

39. Friedlaender, *Approaches to Controlling Air Pollution*, p. 3.

40. The Domestic Council Review Group on Regulatory Reform, "The Challenge of Regulatory Reform" (Washington D.C.: The White House,

January 10, 1977), pp. 59-65. For another view on regulatory reform, see Roger G. Noll, *Reforming Regulation* (Washington, D.C.: The Brookings Institution, 1971).

41. Louis L. Jaffee, "Basic Issues: An Analysis," *New York University Law Review* (1955), p. 1285.

42. See Richard F. Elmore, "Organizational Models of Social Program Implementation," *Public Policy* (Spring 1978), pp. 185-228.

43. James Q. Wilson, *Varieties of Police Behavior* (New York: Atheneum, 1973), p. 3.

44. Richard B. Stewart, "Judging the Imponderables of Environmental Policy" in Friedlaender, *Approaches*, pp. 68-137.

45. Marc J. Roberts and Susan O. Farrel, "The Political Economy of Implementation: The Clean Air Act and Stationary Sources," ibid., pp. 152-81.

46. Jeffrey L. Pressman and Aaron B. Wildavsky, *Implementation: How Great Expectations in Washington Are Dashed in Oakland* (Berkeley, Calif.: University of California Press, 1973), p. 93.

47. Ibid., p. 118.

48. See Edward Banfield, *Political Influence* (New York: The Free Press, 1961), pp. 307-24.

PART I

CHOOSING AN ENVIRONMENTAL POLICY

1

The White House: Idealism Tempered

The focus in the first part of this book is on the policymakers in the White House and Congress who formulated the instructions that EPA received at the time of its creation. The Domestic Council, a unit in the Nixon White House led, in 1969, by John Erlichman, organized a task force that made the initial proposal ultimately resulting in the creation of EPA. This Domestic Council task force, directed by John Whitaker, had been ordered to prepare the "President's Message on the Environment," delivered on February 10, 1970.[1] It proposed that environmental protection and natural resource programs should be combined in a new Department of National Resources.

This proposal was not entirely new. It earlier had been applied to natural resource and environmental programs during the New Deal by the National Resources Planning Board. In 1948, the Hoover Commission also had called for a reorganization of the Interior Department to achieve comprehensive management of pollution control and natural resource functions. The difference between the previous attempts to combine pollution control and natural resource programs and the Domestic Council task force's proposal, however, was that the latter used the "ecological" concepts that were fashionable in the late 1960s to justify the need for a national growth policy.[2] Its suggestion for reorganization was inspired by a view of human beings as "space voyagers on spaceship earth." The view emphasized preserving the ecobalance and decontaminating an already polluted environment.

The task force's communication to the president noted that although studies for over fifty years had recommended that a Department of Natural Resources be created, the notion had never received support from congressional committees, government bureaus, or special interest groups. According to the task force, increased public support for the goal of environmental quality provided the president with a unique opportunity to overcome the resistance that was ordinarily encountered to reorganization in this area.[3]

The president agreed that the environmental protection and natural resources functions of the federal government were appropriate targets for reorganization. Reorganizing the government, however, was not a task that the president had the time or energy to pursue himself; he, therefore, delegated responsibility to the President's Advisory Council on Executive Organization, better known as the Ash Council.

The Ash Council was created in January 1969 after President Nixon took office. Roy Ash, former Litton Industries executive, was appointed its head. Serving with him were Frederick R. Kappel, former chairman of the board of AT&T; Walter N. Thayer, president of Whitney Communications Corporation; Richard M. Paget, president of the management consulting firm of Cresap, McCormick, and Paget; George P. Baker, retiring dean of the Harvard Business School; and John Connally, former governor of Texas and a practicing lawyer. The Ash Council was planning to make wide-scale changes in the federal structure. It hoped to merge existing departments and agencies and create four "super-departments," one for Community Development, one for Economic Affairs, one for Human Resources, and one for Natural Resources.[4]

Ash, however, was the only member of the council who played an active role in the proceedings that led to EPA's

TABLE 4
The Policymakers in the White House Who Took Part in EPA's Creation

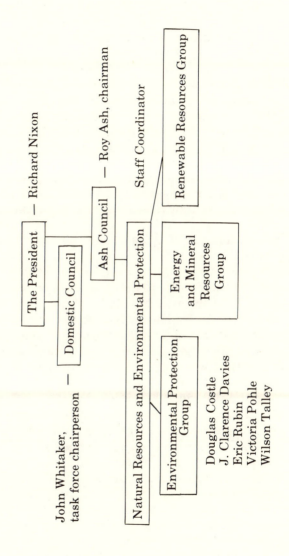

The President — Richard Nixon

John Whitaker,
task force chairperson — Domestic Council

Ash Council — Roy Ash, chairman

Staff Coordinator

Natural Resources and Environmental Protection

Environmental Protection Group

Douglas Costle
J. Clarence Davies
Eric Rubin
Victoria Pohle
Wilson Talley

Energy and Mineral Resources Group

Renewable Resources Group

creation. The others functioned as an absentee board of directors, while the staff that was employed by the council did the actual work of preparing the reorganization. The staff was led by Amory Bradford, a former *New York Times* executive and poverty program official.[5] Bradford also initially favored establishing a Department of Natural Resources. He believed that such a department would respond to the need for a "balanced" growth policy and would conform with the goals of the 1969 National Environmental Policy Act (NEPA). The dictates of NEPA were

to create and maintain conditions under which man and nature can exist in productive harmony, and fulfill the social, economic, and other requirements of present and future generations of Americans.[6]

As stated in the 1970 State of the Union Message, the president's intention was to "develop a national growth policy."[7] The new department, as Bradford envisioned it, would work closely with the recently created Council on Environmental Quality (CEQ), which had been placed in the Executive Office of the president by NEPA. It would develop a growth policy that did not abandon the goal of industrial expansion but changed the emphasis from growth at any price to a policy that was more in harmony with the needs of the ecosystem.

Bradford divided his aides into three groups: an energy and mineral resources group, a renewable resources group, and an environmental protection group. The energy and mineral resources group concentrated on government programs dealing with power production, water supply, and substances mined from the soil; the renewable resources group focused on programs for agriculture, forests, wildlife, and fish; and the environmental protection group had responsibility for waste disposal and pollution control activities.

It was the environmental protection group that played a major role in EPA's creation. The five staff members were: full time council employees Douglas Costle, Victoria Pohle, and Eric Rubin; White House Fellow Wilson Talley in the Department of Health, Education, and Welfare (HEW); and Princeton political science professor J. Clarence Davies.[8] Like Whitaker and Bradford, the members of the environmental protection group believed that the wastes of an "affluent society" should be "comprehensively managed." However, they did not want to see pollution control and natural resource programs combined. Unlike Whitaker and Bradford, the members of this group believed that environmentalists should be represented by an independent agency in the federal structure. Environmentalists should not have to compete with the proponents of industrial development for the attention of the secretary of the proposed Department of Natural Resources.

The environmental protection group introduced a plan to create an independent Environmental Protection Agency responsible only for pollution control, instead of a plan to create a Department of Natural Resources responsible for both pollution control and natural resources functions. The plan, however, was adopted only after it was influenced by the politics of reorganization. The process of reaching agreement between diverse actors produced a more modest reorganization plan than the one originally called for by the Domestic Council task force and a more modest reorganization plan than the one originally envisoned by the environmental protection group. Idealistic impulses were tempered by the political actors who participated in the decision to create an Environmental Protection Agency.

The Arguments of the Environmental Protection Group

Members of the environmental protection group presented three reasons for rejecting the establishment of a Department of Natural Resources and three reasons for accepting instead its proposal to create an Environmental Protection Agency.[9] The following are its reasons for rejecting the proposal to create a Department of Natural Resources:

1. *The task of implementing a national growth policy would be beyond the means of the proposed department.* Decisions about growth involved more factors than the simple trade-off between resource development and environmental protection. Even if pollution control and natural resource programs were consolidated in a single department, it would not combine all the government programs that had an impact on the rate of economic development. Other departments, Housing and Urban Development, Transportation, and Health, Education, and Welfare still would make decisions that affected future economic progress. Their goals had to be balanced alongside of environmental protection. In a Department of Natural Resources oriented toward problems like managing the government-owned lands in the West, city-related and public health factors would not receive the attention they deserved.

2. *The idea of incorporating so many diverse bureaucratic units in a Department of Natural Resources was not politically feasible.* It was unlikely that the various components of a Department of Natural Resources could be broken loose from existing agencies and departments. The congressional committees that had oversight and appropriations responsibility and the constituencies that the existing programs served would not permit a broad reorganization.

3. *A Department of Natural Resources would be a mere "holding company," too large and diverse to be managed effectively.* Even after the numerous resource and environmental programs had been united in a single department, they would be isolated from each other. They would pursue separate goals without effective coordination. A separate environmental protection administration, in contrast, might be able to merge and comprehensively manage the environment and not just consolidate separate pollution control programs.

Three ideas provided a rationale for the group's recommendation to consolidate existing pollution control programs in a separate agency:

1. *New pollution problems that would strain the capacity of the fragmented environmental protection programs then in existence were likely to develop.* An upgraded bureaucratic component directly linked to the president was needed in order

to anticipate problems not yet uncovered. Although scientists knew that pollution was serious, they did not completely grasp the magnitude of the problem. Increases in population, industrial production, mobility, and urbanization would add to already serious environmental problems. The full risk of toxic chemicals, for example, only recently had been detected.[10] Unless a new department or agency with an explicit pollution control mission was created, the federal government would not possess the organizational apparatus it needed to discover new threats and to take on new responsibilities. The failure to consolidate existing pollution control bureaucracies would leave the government unprepared to deal with future damage to the environment.

2. *The functions of pollution control regulation and economic development promotion should be separated.*[11] If pollution control programs were combined with natural resource programs in a Department of Natural Resources, then environmentalists would be overwhelmed by better organized developers. The "fox," as the staff put it, had to be kept out of the "chicken coop." In a Department of Natural Resources, the better organized and financed natural resource interests would tend to prevail over the less well-organized and poorer environmentalists. In such a department when conflicts arose between resource development and pollution control, environmentalists would be likely to lose. Combining the promotion function with the regulatory function would result in a permanent conflict of interest that the secretary of a Department of Natural Resources would have to resolve. On the other hand, such internal conflicts would not afflict the head of an Environmental Protection Agency that was a more single-minded advocate of pollution control.

3. *An integrated and systematic method had to be applied to the problem of managing the unwanted by-products of an "affluent" society.*[12] The government should control as efficiently as possible the total quantity of wastes regardless of the source, media, or form. The interactions among different forms of pollution had to be studied so that standards would be based on the total amount of pollution to which humans and the environment were exposed. An intellectual approach that recognized that the different forms of pollution—air, water, and land—were interchangeable would simplify matters for industries who were guilty of emitting more than one kind of pollution.

BRADFORD AND ASH RESPOND TO THE
ENVIRONMENTAL PROTECTION GROUP'S SUGGESTION

Amory Bradford accepted the arguments made by the environmental protection group against a large department. In the recommendation he transmitted to Ash on March 15, 1970, he maintained that first priority had to be given to the merger of pollution control programs in a separate agency. On April 8, however, Ash turned down this recommendation. Ash's first choice was to bring together related natural resource and environmental functions in a Department of Natural Resources. Ash chose this alternative because his grand design for the entire federal structure involved consolidating departments and reducing the number of officials directly reporting to the president.[13] His theory of reorganization was based on the premise that competing interests had to be united, not separated as members of the environmental protection group believed.

According to Ash, the size of the cabinet had to be reduced. Four "super-departments" (for Community Development, Economic Affairs, Human Resources, and Natural Resources) were needed to rearrange and combine the various programs of the federal government.

Secretaries of large departments were less likely to be advocates of a narrow point of view. Strong, loyal cabinet and subcabinet officials—carefully selected by the president— would be in a position to manage the day-to-day operations of domestic programs, while the Executive Office no longer would be burdened with making the trade-offs between interests represented by competing departments. With fewer officials reporting directly to the White House, the president would be freed from daily operating responsibilities and at the same time in greater control of the bureaucracy.

Ash's convictions were too strong and his plan too well-formulated for him to be influenced by the arguments of the environmental protection group. In this round, he had the final say. Despite the objections of the group and the conversion of Bradford to its point of view, Ash decided against the

TABLE 5

The Proposed Department of Natural Resources

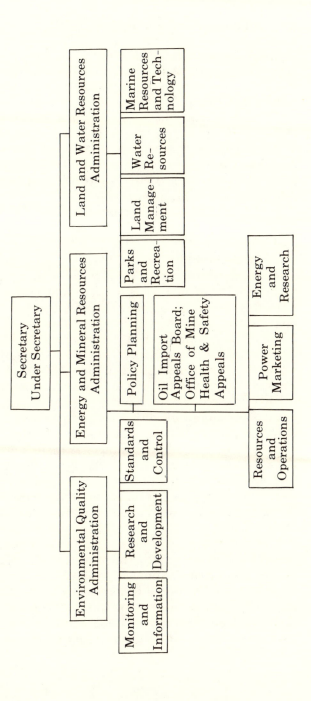

proposal to create an independent Environmental Protection Agency. His proposal to create a Department of Natural Resources would have brought together various pollution control programs, the Atomic Energy Commission (AEC), the Forest Service, the Army Corps of Engineers, and the Department of the Interior.

The proposed Department of Natural Resources would have been the fifth largest department in the federal government, surpassed only by the Departments of Defense, HEW, Argiculture, and Transportation.

Opposition to Ash's Proposal

Ash's proposal, however, had to be cleared by the department heads who would be asked to give up specific programs to the new Department of Natural Resources. On April 9, the day after Ash made his recommendation, council members met with the secretaries of Health, Education, and Welfare (HEW), Housing and Urban Development (HUD), Transportation, Interior, Agriculture, Commerce, and the heads of the Council of Environmental Quality (CEQ) and the Atomic Energy Commission (AEC) to hear their comments.[14]

HEW opposed any reorganization. Representatives of this department maintained that the proponents of reorganization had to demonstrate that the long-term benefits would outweigh the immediate damage. Transfers would disrupt work that was already in progress. Bureaucratic infighting and administrative concerns would dominate during the period of transition. Previous reorganizations had showed that no dramatic improvement in performance was likely to occur.

Commerce Secretary Maurice Stans also opposed any reorganization. Stans raised the problem of integration. He argued that coordination of the different programs in a Department of National Resources would be difficult. Mining, coal, and gas interests would try to prevent consolidation. Different pollution control programs—granted authority by separate statutes, surrounded by diverse interests, and

using different professional groups to perform their tasks—
could not be effectively consolidated. Air pollution, for
instance, was a health problem. It belonged in HEW where
medical research scientists were studying its effects on
health. Water pollution, on the other hand, was a recreation
problem. The purpose was to make waterways more fishable
and swimmable. It belonged in the Department of Interior.

Stans also doubted that the goal of Ash's grand scheme for
the federal bureaucracy, of giving the president greater control, could be met. Control of day-to-day operations would not
be achieved by the cabinet and subcabinet officials of the
proposed Department of National Resources. The department, in Stans' opinion, merely would be an "overgrown"
Department of Interior, a home for diverse and fragmented
programs that had no cohesive purpose.

The secretaries of Agriculture, HUD, and the chairmen of
AEC and CEQ had equally strong reservations about the
feasibility and appropriateness of reorganizing in accord
with Ash's proposal. Agriculture Secretary Hardin mentioned that well-organized farm and chemical industries
would oppose a switch in pesticide responsibility. HUD
Secretary Romney stated that city governments and blacks
would not be pleased with the proposed reorganization. They
would interpret the creation of a Natural Resources Department as an indication that the federal government had abandoned inner-city problems. AEC administrator Seaborg also
opposed the plan because his agency was slated to lose statutory authority to the proposed department.

The only supporters of Ash's proposal were Secretary
Volpe from the Department of Transportation and Secretary
Hickel from the Department of the Interior. Volpe merely
parroted Ash's idea about the need for increased presidential
control of the bureaucracy, but Hickel reiterated the Domestic Council task force's proposition that a Department of
Natural Resources could provide for a "balanced" growth
policy. Hickel's support for the proposal, though, did more to
discredit it than to further its progress. Among Nixon supporters, Hickel was looked upon with disfavor because he

had enthusiastically endorsed Earth Day and publicly criticized the president's environmental record.

THE TURNING POINT

Ash's proposal to create a "super-department" did not have enough support from participating cabinet members. The alternative, to create an independent Environmental Protection Agency, was only actively favored by CEQ. With so much opposition to a Department of Natural Resources and so little support for the alternative, a stalemate was reached. It appeared as if no reorganization would be accomplished. The turning point, however, came when HEW modified its stance. In a discussion paper that it sent to the Ash Council after the April 19 meeting, HEW indicated that it would be willing to support the creation of an independent pollution control agency.[15] Ideally, the paper argued, all environmental programs should be housed in HEW because they were public health programs. Doctors acknowledged that disease was environmentally determined and argued that more health effects research was needed. The drawback to placing all pollution control programs in HEW, however, was the already large size of the department. Lacking visibility in a large department, environmental programs would have trouble competing for funds against other important and growing programs.

The environmental protection group, Bradford, CEQ, and now HEW favored separating the pollution control function from natural resource activities for a similar reason—the need to concentrate resources and attention on the environmental protection problem. Those who were inclined to support a larger department, on the other hand, had very different reasons for doing so. First, the Domestic Council task force and now Hickel viewed a united department as a tool to achieve a "balanced" growth policy, while Ash's primary purpose was to streamline the bureaucracy so that it could be controlled more effectively by the president.

Ash ultimately withdrew his opposition to the staff proposal to create an independent Environmental Protection Agency. In a memorandum to the president on April 29, he advocated the merger of key pollution control programs in a separate agency.

The environmental protection group plan for a separate pollution control agency was presented to the president despite the initial opposition of the Domestic Council task force and of Roy Ash. Part of the reason that the plan for a separate pollution control administration moved successfully through this political obstacle course was that it stood between extremes. On the one hand, the Domestic Council task force and Ash favored the consolidation of *all* natural resource and pollution control programs. On the other hand, HEW, HUD, the Departments of Commerce and Agriculture, and the AEC were opposed to any reorganization. While originally only the environmental protection group and CEQ favored the idea of an independent pollution control agency, in the end, Bradford, HEW, and Ash consented to it. It was a compromise proposal that all of the interested parties could endorse.

The President: Idealism Tempered

In the final reorganization plan that the president submitted to Congress on July 9, he made certain adjustments in the recommendations that Ash sent to him. He appeased cabinet members and agency heads by allowing them to keep programs that they considered necessary for the fulfillment of their departmental missions. The existing departments and agencies did not suffer as large a loss of personnel, resources, and authority as the original Ash Council plan recommended. By not acting on the proposal to create a Department of Natural Resources, Nixon set at ease congressional committees and interest groups that did not want various existing organizational arrangements changed. The Department of Agriculture, for instance, retained the Forest Service; the Department of Defense, the Army Corps of Engineers; and AEC maintained its independent status. By not submitting the plan to establish a Natural Resources Department to Congress and by not taking programs from elsewhere and putting them in EPA, the president calmed the fears of cabinet officials.

However, there was still some anxiety in the White House that EPA would abuse its regulatory powers. Influenced by militant antipollution forces, it might set unreasonable water and air pollution standards that took into account health and ecological factors but did not pay attention to economic cost or technological alternatives. To guard against this possibility, the president adopted a suggestion made by Maurice Stans and strengthened the environmental programs of Department of Commerce. He expanded the environmental research capacity of the department by adding the National Oceanographic and Atmospheric Administration (NOAA) to its programs. While EPA would have around 6,000 employees and a budget of $1.4 billion (80 percent of it construction grant money), NOAA would have nearly 12,000 employees and a budget of $270 million.[16] He carefully balanced the potentially antibusiness EPA with an enhanced environmental program in the probusiness Department of Commerce. If Commerce could challenge EPA's environmental preeminence, then the new agency would be less inclined to promulgate unreasonable standards. The final credit for submitting to Congress the plan to create EPA belongs to Nixon; however, his adjustments had the effect of tempering the idealistic impulses of the plan originally presented by the environmental protection group.

Nixon qualified some of the goals that the designers of the EPA were trying to achieve, but he did not eliminate idealistic purposes entirely. The separation of promotion and regulation was accomplished and the environmentalists could "possess" an agency without having to share it with better organized and better financed resource development interests. Even through EPA was somewhat smaller than its designers had planned, its growth was not necessarily inhi-

TABLE 6
The EPA "Inheritance"

Major Units	Previous Agency	Number of Personnel	Fiscal 1971 Budget (millions)	Administrator
Federal Water Quality Administration	Interior	2,670	1,000	David D. Dominick
Bureau of Water Hygiene	HEW	160	2.3	James McDermott
National Air Pollution Control Administration	HEW	1,100	110	John T Middleton
Bureau of Solid Waste Management	HEW	180	15	Richard D. Vaughan
Pesticides Regulation Division	Agriculture (Agriculture Research Service)	425	5.1	G. G. Rohrer
Office of Pesticides Research	HEW (Food & Drug Administration)	275	10.7	
Research on Effects of Pesticides on Wildlife & Fish	Interior	9	0.216	Raymond E. Johnson
Bureau of Radiological Health	HEW	350	9	John C. Villforth
Federal Radiation Council	Interagency	4	0.144	
Division of Radiation Protection Standards	Atomic Energy	3	0.075	

bited by its initial size. When new pollution problems arose, it could (and did) expand to incorporate them. Furthermore, even through EPA did not receive all environmental programs, it did combine the bulk of federal pollution programs: air and water pollution control activities, pesticides authority, the solid waste program, and some radiation authority.

The theory of comprehensive environmental management was not invalidated. In fact, Nixon's statement about the reorganization stressed the need to merge pollution control functions in order to manage the environment comprehensively.

Despite its complexity, for pollution control purposes the environment must be perceived as a single interrelated system . . . . A single source may pollute the air with smoke and chemicals, the land with solid wastes, and a river or lake with chemical and other wastes. Control of air pollution may produce more solid wastes which then would pollute the land or water. Control of the water polluting effluent may convert it into solid wastes, which must be disposed of on land . . . . A far more effective approach to pollution control would
—Identify pollutants
—Trace them through the entire ecological chain, observing and recording changes in form as they occur
—Determine the total exposure of man and his environment
—Examine interactions among forms of pollution
—Identify where on the ecological chain interdiction would be more appropriate.[17]

In the Nixon administration, the idealistic impulses of the Domestic Council task force and environmental protection group were tempered by counteracting pressures and the need for compromise. This tempering of idealistic impulses, however, did not deprive them of all their vigor.[18] The ideas, principles, and values of EPA's designers were sharpened by the balancing tendencies of political argument. They were honed by the conflict between opposing interests and made more precise by exposure to competing notions. Three examples can be cited. First, the Domestic Council task force's view that an opportune moment existed to overcome the normal resistance of bureaus, agencies, and special interests to large-scale reorganization was tested when the affected departments and the AEC actually were consulted. These consultations revealed the limits to the shifts and transfers that could be made even at an opportune moment. Second, Ash's proposal for a "super-department" of natural resources was based on his scheme to streamline the bureaucracy and to give the president more control over it. His proposal was challenged by Maurice Stans's argument about manageability. The president, according to Stans, could not effectively exert control through a "super-department," because the secretary of such a department would have difficulty consolidating and coordinating such a diverse empire. The third example that can be cited was the Domestic Council's suggestion (shared by others) that the new environmental quality department should be an instrument for a "balanced" growth policy. This suggestion was contested by the environmental protection group's claim that setting a growth policy was beyond the means of a department that united only natural resource and pollution control functions. The political debate and criticism that surrounded the Ash Council proceedings generated a proposal for an agency with a more circumscribed pollution control function and a more attainable environmental protection mission.

Summary

Although there was some quibbling from congressmen, the proposal to create a new pollution control agency that the president submitted on July 9, 1970, was never in serious danger of being rejected. Almost all of the departments actively supported it. Agriculture and AEC testified on its behalf, while HEW did more than just testify. It organized a special task force to lobby among congressmen and to influence the public health constituency. In September 1970, the sixty days required for congressional rejection of a reorganization order expired, and three months later EPA began operations.

The policymaking process in the instance of this reorganization proposal was complex. The steps between the initiation of the proposal to create a Department of Natural Resources and final promulgation of the order to create an Environmental Protection Agency involved the (1) development of a counterproposal by the environmental protection group; (2) Bradford's acceptance of the counterproposal; (3) Ash's initial rejection of the counterproposal; (4) his change of mind after the submission of the original proposal to the heads of departments and agencies; (5) the ensuing stalemate and turning point when HEW changed its position; and (6) the final modifications made by the president. The politics of policy choice involved making a proposal, making a counterproposal, rejecting the counterproposal, not clearing the original proposal with department secretaries and agency heads, accepting the counterproposal, and changing the counterproposal in accord with the wishes of the president.

From the perspective of the rules of classic decision-making, policymaking was not carried out according to rational prescriptions. The process of policy choice was political not analytical. The problem was not carefully defined; goals were not discussed; alternatives were not systematically examined; and the final choice was not the optimal organizational arrangement for attaining desired ends, but an acceptable plan to which the relevant actors consented.

Although decision-making was not rational, the actors involved gave reasons, sometimes lengthy ones, for the positions they adopted. Arguments were made and reasons given about whether to create a Department of Natural Resources or to create an Environmental Protection Agency. The two proposals were fairly carefully considered by a variety of participants, but there was no exhaustive listing of alternatives and comparison of outcomes. The outcome, although not arrived at by rational means, was innovative, given the suggestions and proposals available at the time. The notion of comprehensive environmental management that was used by the president in the reorganization order to create an Environmental Protection Agency was in accord with what various policy analysts had been advocating. A group of economists working under Allen Kneese, for instance, focused on the flow of materials from the environment to the economy and the return flow of these materials back to the environment as wastes or residuals. Kneese and his associates developed a model that tried to provide a "comprehensive view of the environment and the economy." They held that

the comprehensive view of the environment and the economy ... warns against taking an overly narrow and partial view of the pollution problem. Air, water, and solid waste pollution cannot be considered separate, unrelated problems.

The Kneese model implied that there were four options for controlling pollution: (1) reducing the rate of materials and energy input; (2) treating residuals to make them less harmful to the environment; (3) choosing the time and place of discharge so as to minimize damage; and (4) augmenting the waste assimilative capacity of the environment through investment. Kneese's model was implicit in the reorganization plan that created the Environmental Protection Agency.[19]

Notes

1. Council on Environmental Quality, *Environmental Quality: The First Annual Report* (Washington, D.C.: U.S. Government Printing Office, 1970), pp. 254-71. Serving on this task force were government lawyers John Quarles and Roger Strelow, scientist John Buckley, and OMB Budget Examiner Al Alm—all of whom later became leading executives in EPA. See John Whitaker's account of the task force's activities and the creation of EPA in his *Striking a Balance: Environment and Natural Resources Policy in the Nixon-Ford Years* (Washington, D.C.: American Enterprise Institute, 1976).

2. A provocative, popular work on the relationship between ecology and environmental problems is Barry Commoner, *The Closing Circle* (New York: Knopf, 1971). Ecology demands "systems thinking" in the place of ordinary "Descartian logic." Instead of examining the simple cause and effect relationships between discreet entities, ecologists examine the complex connections between living and nonliving matter that are needed to

sustain the ecosystem. According to Commoner, "The First Law of Ecology" is "Everything Is Connected to Everything Else." See pp. 29-36; see also Edward J. Kormondy, *Concepts of Ecology*, 2nd ed. (Englewood Cliffs, N.J.: Prentice-Hall, 1976); Edward J. Kormondy, ed., *Readings in Ecology* (Englewood Cliffs, N.J.: Prentice-Hall, 1965); Paul Ehrlich, Anne Ehrlich, and John Holdren, *Human Ecology: Problems and Solutions* (San Francisco: W. H. Freeman, 1973); Sterling Brubaker, *To Live on Earth* (Baltimore: John Hopkins, 1972); Carol Purcell, ed., *From Conservation to Ecology* (New York: Crowell, 1973); Roderick Nash, ed., *The American Environment: Readings in the History of Conservation* (Reading, Mass.: Addison-Wesley, 1968); Lynton Keith Caldwell, *Environment: A Challenge to Modern Society* (New York: Doubleday, 1971); Lynton Keith Caldwell, *Man and His Environment: Policy and Administration* (New York: Harper & Row, 1975); Roger Revelle and Hans H. Landsberg, eds., *America's Changing Environment* (Boston: Beacon Press, 1967); and William Ophuls, *Ecology and the Politics of Scarcity* (San Francisco: W. H. Freeman, 1977).

3. See Richard Polenberg, "The New Deal and Administrative Reform" and Keith M. Henderson, "Federal Administrative Reorganization 1940-1970," in *Research in the Administration of Public Policy*, ed. Frank Evans and Harold T. Pinkett (Washington, D.C.: Howard University Press, 1975), pp. 97-115.

4. Richard Nathan, "The Administrative Presidency," *The Public Interest* (Summer 1976), pp. 42-45. See also Richard Nathan, *The Plot That Failed: Nixon and the Administrative Presidency* (New York: Wiley, 1975).

5. Bradford is a central character in Jeffrey Pressman and Aaron Wildavsky's account of the Economic Development Administration in Oakland. See *Implementation: How Great Expectations in Washington Are Dashed in Oakland* (Berkeley, Calif.: University of California Press, 1973).

6. This law can be found in *Environmental Quality: The First Annual Report*, pp. 243-50.

7. Ibid., pp. 264-71.

8. See unpublished paper by Douglas Costle, "The Environmental Protection Agency, Its Origin and Role." After serving as head of the Connecticut Environmental Protection Agency, Mr. Costle joined the staff of the Congressional Budget Office. In 1977, President Carter appointed Costle head of the Environmental Protection agency. In 1975, Talley became assistant administrator for research and development at the EPA. Mr. Davies was an invaluable source of information for this study. He has served as a scholar at Resources for the Future in Washington and is now executive vice president of the Conservation Foundation.

9. The list of reasons for rejecting the Department of Natural Resources proposal and accepting instead a proposal to create an Environmental Protection Agency comes from the author's close examination of internal environmental protection group files and memoranda and from discussions he had with the participants.

10. In 1971, the CEQ first proposed that a toxic substances control act be legislated by Congress, but the bill did not pass both houses until 1976. The Toxic Substances Act enables the government to control the companies that produce the synthetic organic compunds that are used to make fibers, plastics, detergents, pesticides, etc. It permits regulation of such substances as asbestos and mercury as well as vinyl chloride, polychlorinated biphenyls (PCB's) and polybrominated biphenyls (PBB's). See "Toxic Substances Control Act," *Environmental Protection News* (December 1976); and Office of Toxic Substances, EPA, *A Framework for the Control of Toxic Substances: A Compilation of Speeches* (Washington, D.C., April 1975).

11. The distinction between the regulatory function and the promotion function is made by Merle Fainsod, *Government and the American Economy*, 2nd ed. (New York: W. W. Norton, 1948). Also see James Q. Wilson, "The Rise of the Bureaucratic State," *The Public Interest* (Fall 1975), pp. 77-103. Harold Seidman, who served as a consultant for the Ash Council, is an advocate of a "competitive approach" to bureaucratic reform that maintains that competing interests have to be included within the administrative structure of the federal government so that no powerful segment of society is either excluded from participation or from gaining an equitable share of the benefits. See Harold Seidman, *Politics, Position and Power* (New York: Oxford University Press, 1970), pp. 3-37, 271-87. An advocate of a similar "competitive approach" is Robert A. Levine of the Rand Corporation, who writes "that bureaucratic operations can be made more effective through competition and competition can be promoted within a bureaucracy by the frequent creation of the new to challenge the old." See Robert A. Levine, *Public Planning: Failure and Redirection* (New York: Basic Books, Inc., 1972), p. 160, chap. 6, "Working with Bureaucracy."

12. See Allen V. Kneese, Robert U. Ayres, Ralph C. D'Arge, *Economics and the Environment: A Materials Balance Approach* (Baltimore: Johns Hopkins, 1970).

13. See Nathan, "The Administrative Presidency," and *The Plot That Failed.*

14. This account of the positions taken by the affected departments and agencies comes from documents in the environmental protection group's files. Also see Whitaker, *Striking a Balance.*

15. The discussion paper was contained in the environmental protection group's documents that the author examined.

16. The NOAA plan had its genesis in the Stratton Commission Report and the very strong pressures to create a separate agency to deal with ocean matters. The political forces and actors involved in the NOAA plan were different from those involved in the EPA plan. Counterbalancing EPA was only one of the motivations for the NOAA plan.

17. This message can be found in *Environmental Quality: The First Annual Report,* pp. 294-305.

18. Contrary political forces also regulated the idealistic inclinations of

the creators of the War on Poverty. In his book *Maximum Feasible Misunderstanding*, Daniel Patrick Moynihan describes a process that he refers to as the "professionalization of reform." Kennedy's election, he writes,

brought to Washington... a striking echelon of persons whose profession might justifiably be described as knowing what ails societies and whose art is to get treatment underway before the patient is aware of anything noteworthy taking place.

Like the creators of the War on Poverty, the designers of EPA can be characterized as "professional reformers." They were among the "striking echelon of persons" still found in Washington after Nixon's election. In the Nixon administration, such persons were just as constrained by countervailing political forces. See Daniel P. Moynihan, *Maximum Feasible Misunderstanding* (New York: The Free Press, 1970).

19.   See A. Myrck Freeman, Joel Haveman, and Allen V. Kneese, *The Economics of Environmental Policy* (New York: Wiley, 1973).

2

Congress: Nader Power

At the same time that the White House was deciding EPA's creation, Congress was choosing a new clean air statute that the new agency would have to implement.[1] The 1970 Clean Air Act along with the 1972 Federal Water Pollution Control Act (which will be discussed in Chapters 5 and 6) were the most significant pieces of legislation that the newly formed EPA would have to enforce, in terms of the statutory powers delegated to it and in terms of the resources and personnel committed to carrying out these acts. In Congress the decision-making process that led to the passage of the Clean Air Act was different from the decision-making process in the White House that led to the birth of EPA. While in the White House the steps between the making of a proposal and the final promulgation of the reorganization order involved a complex process of proposals and counterproposals, in Congress the steps between the making of the original proposal and the final declaration of a new Clean Air Act was marked by an accusation and a response. Senator Edmund Muskie (D.—Maine), a chief architect of the air and water pollution control legislation that had been passed by Congress in the 1960s, was accused by a Nader study group of failing to provide adequate pollution control leadership. This accusation led to Muskie's commitment to a stronger antipollution posture.

The steps in the legislative decision-making process were fewer, the intervening political process was less complex,

TABLE 7
Choosing an Environmental Policy: 1969-70

	Events Leading to EPA Creation	Events Leading to Passage of the 1970 Clean Air Act
Nov. 1969	Domestic Council task force advises Ash Council to combine natural resource and environmental protection programs in a Department of Natural Resources	
Dec. 1969		Muskie introduces a clean air bill that states that air pollution regulations have to be kept within the bounds of technical knowledge and economic feasibility
Feb. 10, 1970	The president announces the Ash council reorganization study	The president proposes national air quality standards to replace regional standards
Mar. 4, 1970		Muskie continues to adhere to the regional air quality approach

TABLE 7
Continued

Events Leading to EPA Creation		Events Leading to Passage of the 1970 Clean Air Act
April 8, 1970	Although the environmental protection group recommends separating natural resource and pollution control functions, Ash proposes combining resource development and pollution control programs in a Department of Natural Resources	
April 9, 1970	Department secretaries and agency heads voice opposition to Department of Natural Resources proposal	
April 29, 1970	Ash Council in memo to the president advocates that key antipollution programs be merged in the Environmental Protection Agency	

TABLE 7
Continued

	Events Leading to EPA Creation	Events Leading to Passage of the 1970 Clean Air Act
May 1970		Appearance of Nader report, *Vanishing Air*
June 10, 1970		Muskie suggests that transportation control plan requirements be included in the new Clean Air Act
July 9, 1970	President submits Reorganization Plan No. 3 (EPA) and No. 4 (NOAA) to Congress	
July-Aug. 1970		Senate pollution control subcommittee drafts a Clean Air Act with national standards, transportation control plan provisions, and strict auto pollution reduction requirements
Sept. 9, 1970	Sixty days for congressional rejection of the	

TABLE 7
Continued

Events Leading to EPA Creation	Events Leading to Passage of the 1970 Clean Air Act
Reorganization Order to expire	

	Events Leading to EPA Creation	Events Leading to Passage of the 1970 Clean Air Act
Nov. 17, 1970		Letter signed by HEW Secretary Elliot Richardson reaches conference committee and urges that auto pollution reduction requirements be relaxed
Dec. 2, 1970	EPA begins operations	
Dec. 18, 1970		Final version of Clean Air Act submitted to Congress
Dec. 31, 1970		President signs Clean Air Act and makes it law

and the changes that occurred between policy initiation and the final declaration of a new clean air policy were different from the policymaking process in the White House. While in the White House, a broad proposal to make a Department of Natural Resources was toned down by intervening politics, in Congress, a less ambitious proposal to make modifications in the old clean air statutes was made more stringent by intervening politics.

The Pollution Control Subcommittee

The Senate Subcommittee on Air and Water Pollution—created within the Public Works Committee in 1963—had nearly seven years of experience with pollution control legislation when it started to draft new clean air amendments in 1970. Since the early 1960s it had developed a knowledgeable staff (headed by Muskie advisor Leon Billings), held many hearings on the pollution problem, created a constituency of independent experts upon whom it called, and worked closely with the National Air Pollution Control Administration (NAPCA) and the other agencies and bureaus that were predecessors to EPA.

In the 1960s as public awareness of the air pollution problem began to rise, the subcommittee modified existing air

TABLE 8
Pre-1970 Air Pollution Legislation*

Date	Title	Provisions
1955	No title	Temporary authority for research, demonstrations, and training
1963	Clean Air Act	National enforcement hearings-conference-court procedure for interstate pollution
1965	Motor Vehicle Air Pollution Control Act	Federal regulation of emissions from new motor vehicles
1966	Clean Air Act Amendments	Maintenance grants for air pollution control agencies
1967	Air Quality Act	Federal-state-standard setting for air quality control regions

*Adapted from J. Clarence Davies III and Barbara S. Davies, *The Politics of Pollution* (Indianapolis: Bobbs-Merrill, 1975), p. 46.

pollution statutes producing a series of broader and more stringent acts. The 1963 Clean Air Act, like the first national air quality pollution authority, which was granted in 1955, called for federal research and training. The federal government also was given limited powers over interstate pollution, and it was directed to study the auto emissions problem. In 1964 a report issued by the Senate subcommittee on the auto emissions problem called for emissions controls on new motor vehicles. According to the Senate version of the 1965 bill, HEW—after giving "appropriate consideration to technological feasibility and economic cost"—was directed to set emissions standards for new motor vehicles by September 1, 1967. The House, however, amended the bill eliminating the statutory deadline. In 1967, the president called for national emissions standards for all industrial sources, but Congress weakened the bill by requiring regional air quality standards. If the federal government had set emissions standards, it would have directly set tolerable levels of pollution for categories of industrial facilities throughout the country. Since it only set regional air quality standards, its control was limited to establishing tolerable levels of air pollution in different regions. Although air pollution laws gradually became more stringent in the 1960s a pattern was already established—Congress weakened legislation before passing it.

Unlike other subcommittee chairmen who drafted laws without much input from the other members of their subcommittees, Muskie tried to take subcommittee member opinion into account and mold it into a final product without imposing his will on the other subcommittee members. The drafting of the 1970 Clean Air Act involved the following six subcommittee members.

Jennings Randolph (D.—W.V.)
John Sherman Cooper (R—K.)
Howard Baker (R—Tenn.)
Thomas Eagleton (D.—Mo.)
J. Caleb Boggs (R.—Del.)
William Spong (D.—Va.)

Baker, an engineer by training, was optimistic that technological advances could be made to control pollution without
major costs to the economy. Eagleton was influenced by his
friendship with Senator Gaylord Nelson, a strong environmentalist and sponsor of Earth Day. Baker and Eagleton,
with their pro-environmental views, were considered the
committee's innovators. Boggs, a rather conservative
Republican, was expected to try to block efforts to legislate
clean air; while Cooper, Spong, and Randolph were cautious
southern Democrats who believed in slow deliberations, fair-
ness, and compromise.

Before the appearance of the Nader report in May 1970, the
plan of the subcommittee was to modify the existing regional
air quality standard setting process.[2] The bill, which Senator
Muskie introduced on December 10, 1969, included a new
public hearing provision but specifically stated that air pollution regulations had to be kept within the bounds of technical knowledge and economic feasibility. In February the
president made a proposal that national air quality standards replace regional standards, but Muskie introduced a
second group of provisions on March 4, 1970, that continued
to adhere to the regional air quality approach. One of these
provisions set a more prompt deadline for the promulgation
of regional standards. The most innovative feature of the
second group of provisions, however, was a citizen suit measure that could be used to enjoin violations of emissions
requirements and require enforcement of air quality goals.
The early drafts of the 1970 Clean Air Amendments indicated that Muskie and his subcommittee were only willing to
do minor tinkering with the 1967 law, but were not willing to
alter its provisions fundamentally.

Nader's Influence and Muskie's Vulnerability

In drafting the Clean Air Act, the media focused on Senator Muskie at a critical juncture when the pressure on him
from the House of Representatives, the White House, and
public opinion to make more extensive revisions of the old

clean air statutes was building. The media publicized accusations hurled at the senator by a Nader study group. The publication of the Nader study group's report *Vanishing Air* in 1970, an accusation that received media coverage, evoked a commitment to a stronger posture from Muskie.[3] The report accused Muskie of not taking a "tough" stand against private industry, and the media gave this criticism of an aspiring presidential candidate, extensive coverage.[4] The media stories stressed the study group's accusations that Muskie had "sold out" to industry interests.[5] These charges made Muskie indignant. At the press conference the day after the report appeared, he maintained that his subcommittee had not acted "for the dark, secret, conspiratorial reasons" suggested by the Nader report. He criticized those who adopted a tactic of "excessive confrontation" and promised to strengthen the air pollution laws before the end of the year.[6]

According to Charles O. Jones' account of the incident, "... the overall effect put Muskie in the position of having to do something extraordinary in order to recapture his [pollution control] leadership."[7] Before the Nader report appeared, Muskie supported retention of regional control over air quality standards.

After the Nader report was published, however, Muskie agreed to national standards for major pollutants.[8] He also changed his approach to the air pollution amendments in three additional ways: he favored standards based on health and welfare criteria that would not be influenced by considerations of economic or technological feasibility; he supported regulations that would make the auto manufacturers reduce carbon monoxide, hydrocarbon, and nitrogen oxide emissions 90 percent in five years; and he called for the use of traffic control plans that would eliminate automobile use in some parts of major cities.

From the issuance of the Nader report in May 1970 until the conference committee delivered the final version of the Clean Air Act to Congress in December, Muskie tried to construct a law that took a "tough" stand against private industry and had stringent enforcement provisions associated with it.[9]

After the Nader report appeared, Muskie recommended that the senators in his subcommittee search for "handles" to force industry to achieve air quality goals by a specific date. Under Muskie's direction, the subcommittee drafted clean air amendments that accepted national quality goals, added stringent provisions to control motor vehicle pollution, introduced the concept of transportation control, and made use of deadlines to achieve progress by a specific date. The Nader report helped push the senator and his subcommittee beyond the incremental adjustments they had been considering.

James Q. Wilson explains Nader's influence on the consumer and environmental protection bills that were passed in the late 1960s and early 1970s as a "symbiotic political relationship" that developed between "public interest" activists and subcommittee chairmen who were interested in gaining national prominence.[10] He cites the example of auto safety legislation where Senator Abraham Ribicoff and his Subcommittee on Executive Reorganization worked together with Nader against the auto manufacturers to pass auto safety legislation. While this theory of a "symbiotic relationship" may apply to the passage of other consumer and environmental protection laws, it does not fit the case of the 1970 Clean Air Amendments. In this instance Senator Muskie's subcommittee and the Nader task force were antagonists and not collaborators.

In contrast to the theory of convergence of interest between public interest activists and congressmen, Simon Lazarus suggests that Nader wields power by shaming officials and appealing to the public's sense of outrage.[11] He maintains that Nader attacks the credibility and reputation of public figures because "accusation invites coverage."[12] The more shocking the accusation the more media attention it attracts. According to Richard Leone, "Public interest groups are dependent on shock techniques.... Extra headlines are brought about only by controversy and response."[13]

The Nader report's influence on the passage of the new Clean Air Act in 1970 depended upon the receptiveness of the media to the report's charges. Some have argued that the media cooperated with Nader because of the information he and his researchers gathered. Mark Nadel, for instance, observes that Nader was "the focal point for a fluctuating informational network."[14] When reporters or broadcasters wanted to understand technical issues, such as new marketing restrictions, or wanted to know particular statistics about health or safety risks, they called on Nader and his public interest groups. Nader and the groups he created provided journalists with information that they did not have the time to gather by themselves.

Others have mentioned that the "audacity" of the Nader reports attracted media coverage.[15] While journalists often romanticize the role of muckraker and express cynicism about the government process, in carrying out their daily assignments they have to appear objective and nonpartisan. Their job is to report the information that the parties involved in a story provided them. For instance, they cannot report as fact that the Federal Trade Commission was a "lethargic pawn of lobbyists" and expect their report to be published, but they can write that Nader or a member of his task force made this assertion. Nader and his study groups then run "interference for timid journalists."[16] The journalists' intentions to uproot corruption are hidden behind the cover of quotations from Nader or one of his associates.

While these explanations of the close ties between Nader and the media are worthy of consideration, they fail to take into account that Nader and his study groups attacked vulnerable targets. Senator Muskie was vulnerable for at least three reasons. First, he was being considered as a potential presidental candidate; second, the 1967 Air Quality Act, which he had helped draft, was not being administered successfully; and finally, the House and the president were challenging his pollution control leadership.

In the year that public concern about pollution control was growing rapidly, Muskie's expertise and experience in the pollution control area made him an attractive presidential candidate. In fact, the national exposure gained as vice-presidential candidate in 1968 made Muskie the front-runner among Democratic contenders. His activities therefore were scrutinized carefully by influential reporters who covered national issues. The Nader report tried to take advantage of the vulnerabilities of this potential presidential candidate. It prodded Muskie for his presidential ambitions and questioned his character and motives.[17] The authors of *Vanishing Air* wondered if a presidential contender had the time to provide proper pollution control leadership in the Senate.

Muskie was also vulnerable because the 1967 Air Quality Act that he had helped draft had not been successfully implemented.[18] The provisions of this act were complicated. Based on a regional approach, the 1967 act gave the states 90 days after the federal government issued criteria documents to file a letter of intent stating that within 180 days they would establish standards for that pollutant. The criteria documents were scientific descriptions of the health effects that would occur if the ambient air level of a pollutant exceeded a certain figure. However there was no deadline in the law for the publication of the criteria documents, and they had no force as law. They were simply guidelines, sources of information to assist the states in the setting of air quality standards. Criteria describe the effects of different levels of pollutants. Thus "X parts per million of sulfur dioxide will produce lung irritation in human beings" is a health criteria. A welfare criteria is a more ambiguous category.[19] In addition to "primary" health-based standards, the 1970 Clean Air Act required "secondary" air quality standards that "protect the public welfare from any known or anticipated effects of air pollutants..."[20] A welfare criteria is any other known or anticipated effect associated with the presence of the pollutant besides the adverse health impact.

After the adoption of ambient standards the states had another 180 days to develop *implementation plans*. The implementation plan was supposed to indicate the maximum amount of emissions that would be permitted from a specific source and also establish a timetable for the enforce-

ment of these emission standards. As of March 1, 1970—
more than two years after the act had been passed—no
criteria documents had been issued, and no state had a full-
scale standards implementation plan in effect for any
pollutant.[21]

The Nader report accused Muskie of being responsible for
passing a cumbersome and weak bill that could not be
enforced properly. It made the charge that Muskie, unlike
such figures as Vice President Humphrey and Secretary of
HEW Gardner, had supported state programs and had not
emphasized the need for an expanded federal role. Muskie
was to blame according to the Nader report because in 1967
he did not support the bill that Lyndon Johnson sent to
Congress that called for national emissions standards, stating how much industries throughout the country could pollute. In contrast, the health and welfare standards that
Muskie supported only required that the federal government
set standards that would state how much pollution the environment in a particular region could absorb.

The Nader report intimated that by opposing national
emissions standards and backing a regional air quality
scheme, Muskie was guilty of "selling out" to industry. It
noted that Muskie and his subcommittee held a series of
informal meetings with industry representatives before public discussion on the bill began. At the public hearings, the
Nader report argued that both Muskie and industry had the
same anti-emissions standard position.[22] The coal industry
had the support of Jennings Randolph (D.—W.V.), a member
of Muskie's subcommittee and chairman of the full Public
Works Committee. Randolph was worried that emissions
standards would force many industries and utilities that
used coal to switch to cleaner burning fuels. According to the
Nader report, Muskie's position was not that much different
from Randolph's.[23] Both represented the views of American
industry. There was a "silent, unspoken unanimity" that
nothing should be done to support "bold legislation to control
pollution."[24]

A final aspect of Muskie's vulnerability was that members of the House of Representatives and the White House were attacking the existing air pollution program even before the Nader report appeared.[25] The catalyst in the House was Representative Paul Rogers (D—Fl.), the second ranking member of the House Subcommittee on Public Health and Welfare. During public hearings that he convened in December 1969, he showed dissatisfaction with the existing air pollution statutes. The president's message on the environment presented to Congress on February 10, 1970, made numerous proposals to change the statutes that Muskie had helped author.[26] Among the most important of the president's proposals was a call for national air quality standards, a suggestion that Muskie had explicitly rejected. The administration bill required that EPA set national air quality standards within six months after the bill's passage. On June 3, 1970, the House Committee on Foreign and Interstate Commerce approved a more stringent bill that would have required the agency to set air quality standards thirty days after the bill was passed. The call by Rogers and the president for national air quality standards to be promulgated in a short period of time challenged Muskie's leadership as the initiator and drafter of new pollution control legislation.

Muskie's vulnerability only heightened the influence of *Vanishing Air*. Another reason for the influence of the Nader report was that it simplified controversial issues in order to convey an unambiguous message. Two of its simplifications stand out and will be noted. First, the Nader report gave only a partial rendering of the debate concerning regional versus national standards. Second, its criticism of the delay in issuing criteria documents did not take into account problems of judgment in a case where the scientific evidence was (and is) uncertain.

Muskie had a legitimate defense for his continued endorsement of regional air quality standards. In 1967 he was opposed to national air quality standards because the administration proposed that they be based on technological achievability. Since this knowledge had to be derived from industrial sources, Muskie feared that national emissions standards that conformed to this criteria would be unnecessarily low. He favored health-based regional air quality standards because they were "technology-forcing." Health-based standards in Muskie's opinion created a sense of public urgency that pushed industry beyond the technology it had been using.

Regional-based standards had another advantage over national standards. In Muskie's opinion, they permitted the focus to be on particular problem areas where states were more likely to adopt standards more stringent than those of the federal government. While national standards might be set at the lowest common level, some localities were likely to want to establish more demanding goals. For example, in Pittsburgh stricter standards might be adopted than in the farmlands of Nebraska. Under a regional approach, Muskie believed that areas with severe air pollution problems would be able to enact more ambitious programs than a universal one adopted by the federal government.

California was the example that Muskie often cited. This state had led the nation in air pollution developments,[27] by making the first serious effort to control auto pollution. In 1959, the California state legislature ordered the Director of Public Health to conduct research into vehicular air pollution, and in 1960 California was the first state to promulgate auto pollution standards. The California state government progressively tightened its auto pollution standards as technology for better emissions control became available. In 1970 the California state senate went so far as to threaten to ban the internal combustion engine by 1975.

Prodded into reducing motor vehicle exhaust pollution by the stricter air quality goals and enforcement program established in California, auto manufacturers had been among the first to call for national emissions standards. In fact, a February 1970 poll of business executives done by *Fortune* magazine showed that 59 percent of the nation's corporate leaders favored national standards because they were afraid of stricter state standards.[28] Far from proving Muskie's lack of "toughness," his acceptance of regional quality goals demonstrated a concern for pushing industry forward technologically and for compelling it to address particularly acute local problems.

Another example of the Nader report's simplifying a controversial topic was its criticism of the handling of the criteria documents by the National Air Pollution Control Administration, a predecessor of EPA.[29] Establishing levels of pollution dangerous to health was (and is) a complicated process because the scientific evidence on the harm caused by pollution is ambiguous.[30] *Vanishing Air* emphasized indirect evidence that linked air pollution and cancer; but it failed to mention that none of the major air pollutants (hydrocarbons, carbon monoxide, nitrogen oxides, sulfuric oxide, and particulates) was a *proven* carcinogen. The report did not take into account that air pollution is not a direct cause of illness. Although incidents have occurred in London, New York, and other cities where the death rate from heart disease, bronchitis, and emphyszema rose rapidly during severe air pollution episodes (known as inversions), these incidents of rising death rates are explained by the death of people already incapacitated to some degree by weak hearts or lungs. In addition, although certain areas of the country have been called "death row" because of the epidemiological evidence linking cancer and air pollution, the evidence that air pollution leads to a high death rate in these areas is circumstantial because it does not isolate variables sufficiently to make definitive statements about cause and effect. The high "death rate" might be attributed to crowding, poor sanitation, nervous tension, or other factors that epidemiological studies cannot control. The links that are suggested by the epidemiological evidence between air pollution and particular illnesses are not the same as the causal links that have been established in the laboratory between particular germs and viruses and particular diseases. Ultimately, the most that can be said about health risks is that air pollution contributes to a gradual decline in general cellular wellbeing.

Crucial questions still need to be answered before credible criteria can be established. There has been no experimental way of estimating the harm caused by the synergestic effect of many pollutants operating simultaneously, and there has been no definitive determination of the threshold of air pollution concentration beyond which negative health effects occur. Without answers to these questions, criteria documents have to be based on "informed judgment." For the National Air Pollution Control Administration, delay was a reasonable maneuver given the scientific uncertainty that exists. *Vanishing Air* did not take into account these problems of judgment that exist under conditions of scientific uncertainty.

The Nader report's simplification of controversial issues was well attuned to the media's definition of a "good story." It focused on an "evil" personified by polluting industries, an ineffectual bureaucracy, and the unfortunate victims of pollution.[31] It evoked "horror stories" which exaggerated the virtue of those who were to benefit and the wickedness of those who were to bear the burden; but it did not take into account the costs of meaningful enforcement in a case where the scientific knowledge was uncertain.[32] Since the media tended to "view public affairs as a species of athletic contest," there was a "bit of theatrics" involved in the way that the Nader report aroused the public's indignation.[33]

Lacking the wealth, organization, and specialized information possessed by industry, the Nader task force needed to cultivate good relations with the media in order to exert influence. To defeat a small group of regulated industries faced with the immediate prospect of increased financial burdens resulting from stringent emissions controls, it had to convince a large number of unorganized individual citizens, each of whom might benefit, if at all, only in the future.[34] The task force's influence depended upon its ability to use the politics of public persuasion to arouse this large and diverse group. It had to act the roles of publicist and popularizer, providing simple emotionally charged information to private citizens who usually lacked interest and knowledge about regulatory issues. To do so, it chose a vulnerable target and simplified controversial issues.

Drafting the 1970 Clean Air Act

The Nader task force influenced the character of the 1970 air pollution legislation not by collaborating with subcomittee chairman Muskie but by publicly rebuking him. Its tactics affected the senator because they attracted media coverage. The task force adopted an adversary relationship toward Muskie, and his subcommittee and the senator and his colleagues in turn adopted an adversary relationship toward industry and the bureaucracy. In response to the attack by the Nader task force, Muskie and his subcommittee became committed to a "tough" posture and a "stern response." The subcommittee sessions that started in July 1970 and lasted until August 4 focused on finding what Muskie referred to as "handles" to pin the bureaucracy and industry to specific air pollution goals.

These "handles" also addressed a problem that scholars of regulatory administration have called "vague delegation of authority." In a study entitled *Reforming Regulation*, Roger Noll explains lack of goal achievement by regulatory agencies in terms of vague delegation.

Most [regulatory] agencies were established through bad legislation that did not adequately define the role and responsibility of the regulators.[35]

According to this explanation, the typical regulatory statute has indefinite provisions. In effect, Congress says to the bureaucracy, "Here is the problem—deal with it." (In some cases, Congress does not know what the problem is and says, "Discover the problem and deal with it.")[36] The agency does not have the nondiscretionary authority it needs to coerce industry and the public into achieving statutory goals.

In 1955 Marver Bernstein suggested that vague statutory language was one of the reasons for the "capture" of regulatory agencies by business.[37] Drawing upon existing legal literature about delegation of authority to regulatory agencies, he argued that the character of the law affected an agency's relationship to the businesses it tried to control: The vaguer the laws that the agency administered, the less likely that the agency would be independent of the businesses it was supposed to govern. In 1969, Theodore Lowi brought together much of the scholarly criticism of vague legislation in a chapter in his book *The End of Liberalism*.[38] Lowi relied heavily on the works of law school Professor Kenneth Culp Davis and former FCC commissioner (and later federal judge) Henry J. Friendly. These authors stressed the problems of undefined discretion in government agencies. The remedy for agency problems attributable to vague and ill-informed legislation was statutes drafted by Congress that had clear goals and explicit means of implementation. Statutes of this character would institutionalize and make binding the sentiments of the public originally mobilized for the purpose of passing the legislation. Armed with strict legal authority, a regulatory agency was less likely to perform inadequately, even if its activities no longer commanded general interest or attention.

"Handles," therefore, served two purposes: the needs of Muskie and his subcommittee to appear "tough" on industry and the needs of regulatory reformers who wanted legislators to establish clear means and goals for controlling industrial behavior. The senators serving on Muskie's subcommittee made use of three "handles": (1) deadlines; (2) national health and welfare goals; and (3) emissions standards.

At the early subcommittee session the senators discussed the implications of a deadline strategy and agreed to accept it. Senator Eagleton had worked on coal mine safety legislation and proposed that the Muskie subcommittee copy its use of timetables. Eagleton argued that timetables would push industry and the bureaucracy forward and make them more accountable to Congress and the public.

While there was unanimity about the use of deadlines, the senators disagreed about a requirement for national or regional air quality goals. Boggs and Baker sought national air quality goals, while Muskie tended to favor the regional approach. Boggs suggested a compromise—that there be separate health *and* welfare goals: the health standards would be established by the national government and would be minimum levels that applied everywhere in the country; the welfare standards would vary from state to state depending upon what values the states wanted to emphasize and how far they wanted to go in the direction of improving their air quality. Muskie agreed and the statute was written with a distinction between nationally based health standards and regionally based welfare standards in mind.

National emissions standards as proposed by the Nader report, however, were rejected. Muskie chose health-based air quality goals over emissions standards because he considered the former to be a better "handle" to use against industry.[39] He believed industry would have less ability to challenge health-based air quality standards than emissions standards based on possible technological achievements or economic cost. Data on possible achievements and cost had to be derived from industry sources, and such data were likely to favor only slight modifications of the status quo. Health-based standards established by the bureaucracy, on the other hand, were a useful political tool to get industry moving. They were a technology-forcing provision. Muskie had confidence in health-based standards because NAPCA scientists had been working on criteria documents since 1967 and had arrived at reasonable figures with which to establish legal watersheds of what was permissible and what was not permissible.

The subcommittee rejected the national industrial emissions standards but strengthened its commitment to controlling motor vehicle emissions. Since 1965, the federal government had the authority to set automobile emissions standards.[40] However, the 1970 amendments went well beyond the provisions of the earlier 1965 act. The 1970 act mandated that the auto companies had to make a 90 percent reduction in hydrocarbons and carbon monoxide by 1975 and a 90 percent reduction in nitrogen oxide emissions by 1976. The bureaucracy no longer had the discretion to decide when it would issue emissions limitations and how strict these limitations would be.

THE NINETY PERCENT REDUCTION REQUIREMENT

The requirement that a 90 percent reduction had to be made in five years proved to be one of the most controversial provisions of the 1970 Clean Air Act.[41] The question asked by Jacoby and Steinbruner is why Congress required the automobile companies to achieve a 90 percent reduction in five years when add-on devices like the catalytic converter would be needed.[42] Add-on devices were expensive to produce and maintain and easy to unhook. Were the manufacturers to adopt instead a ten-year time frame, a new engine (such as stratified charge, diesel, or Rankine) could be developed.[43] The 1975 deadlines, on the other hand, forced the auto companies to rely on a catalytic converter that had to be used with the standard internal combustion engine. Why did Congress make this decision?

In a *Public Interest* article Howard Margolis suggested that this decision was made because Muskie and the pollution control subcommittee arranged a compromise between the auto companies, who wanted to preserve the internal combustion engine, and environmentalists, who favored banning this engine.[44] The auto companies received a substantive victory by retaining the internal combustion engine and the environmentalists achieved a symbolic victory by passing a bill with strict provisions.

The theory that Muskie insisted on the five-year/90 percent reduction because it was a suitable compromise between the auto manufacturers and environmentalists hinges on the assumption that industry, if it was not actively seeking this compromise, was a willing participant in the bargaining process; but the record demonstrates that industry actively opposed the 90 percent reduction. During the conference committee sesssions, the auto manufacturers intervened through

HEW Secretary Richardson and tried to move the 1975-76 deadlines to 1980-81.[45] A letter signed by Richardson reached the conference on November 17 and urged that the deadlines be relaxed. The letter, the work of an administrative task force located primarily in OMB, had been influenced by Maurice Stans, secretary of commerce and Lloyd Cutler, Washington lawyer and auto company lobbyist. Under Muskie's leadership, the conference committee did not "cave-in" to this pressure, but it added a major loophole. The auto companies could apply for a one-year extension of the 1975 and 1976 deadlines.

The theory that Muskie and the subcommittee compromised competing demands assumes that the senator and his subcommittee chose the catalytic converter to save the existing technology; but the subcommittee and Muskie were aware of the pitfalls of the catalytic converter. A July 22 memo produced by Muskie's staff questioned the extent to which the converter could hold up in operation, the value of the rare metals used in the converter, and the costs of installing the converter.

In interviews, Muskie maintained that he did not favor either the internal combustion engine or alternatives to the internal combustion engine. He believed that both technologies, add-on devices and alternatives, had to be explored. Why then did the senator and the subcommittee require the 90 percent reduction in five years? They had objections to allowing industry another ten years to develop a new technology because they felt that the companies had previously used the promise of a clean engine as a delaying tactic.[46] What they considered important was that government apply pressure to get industry moving. The extra time industry had to resolve uncertainties would permit more automobiles to be manufactured without pollution control devices. Further delays would endanger the public health. On the other hand, a five-year deadline, even if technologically infeasible, would force the auto manufacturers to reduce pollution as fast as they could by whatever means available.[47] The impetus behind the 1970 Clean Air Act originally was anti-auto manufacturers and pro-environmentalists, but in the long run industry may have benefited by prolonging the life of the conventional engine.

Muskie's pride in the "strong, tough" air pollution legislation he helped draft was evident in the statement accompanying the bill that he sent to the two houses on December 18, 1970.

I commend...the result of the conferees' painstaking efforts over the past three months. It is a strong, tough, air pollution control agreement. It will enable the country to clean up the air and protect the public health....

This measure—had unanimous support from the Senate conferees—
...*all of whom knew that a public demand needed a stern* response-
...The key decision, the one on which the committee focused most over the past few months, was the deadline for the cleaning up of the internal combustion engine....

The deadline has been retained. That deadline is January 1, 1975, for carbon monoxide and hydrocarbons, and January 1, 1976, for oxides of nitrogen. *I repeat, that deadline has been retained.*[48]

A public accusation elicited Muskie's commitment to stringent legislation, and he did not want to suggest in any way that he was making any deals with industry.[49]

Summary

The pollution control subcommittee had been accustomed to making relatively incremental changes in air pollution control legislation, and only gradually expanded legal authority from a research program into interstate enforcement, auto emissions limitations, and regional air quality standards. In 1965 the subcommittee let the bureaucracy decide when and if it would issue motor vehicle emissions standards, and in 1967, it rejected a White House proposal to authorize national emissions standards for all industrial sources. The appearance of the Nader report in May 1970—after Representative Paul Roger's subcommittee on Public

Health and Welfare had criticized NAPCA for delay and the president had proposed that national air quality goals be put into effect—upset the usual inclination of the subcommittee to make merely incremental adjustments.

After the appearance of the Nader report, the search began for "handles" that would force industry to make progress and compel it to achieve goals. Muskie and the Senate pollution subcommittee decided on deadlines, health and welfare standards, and national auto emissions limitations as the "handles" that it used. They did not compromise on demands that alternatives to the internal combustion engine be considered. If the 90 percent reduction gave industry the chance to develop an alternative to the internal combustion engine, the subcommittee did not plan to discourage such a development. What concerned Muskie and the subcommittee was program progress—the achievement of goals by particular dates. Muskie and the subcommitee wanted the bureaucracy held accountable for past failures. The strict requirements in the 1970 Clean Air Act were designed to compel specific progress according to congressionally mandated timetables. Whether or not these goals could be achieved, the five-year/90 percent reduction was designed to provoke a confrontation between industry and Congress and to force industry to reduce pollution as fast as it could by whatever means it could.

Even without the Nader report's accusations, such factors ao the mood of the times, House criticism of the 1967 Air Quality Act, and presidential proposals to increase federal air pollution authority would have forced the pollution control subcommittee to revise the old statutes. Had there been no Nader report, however, the revisions of the subcommittee would have been minor in comparison with the proposals it made after the report's appearance. Before *Vanishing Air* was published, the subcommittee planned to make minor adjustments in the regional air quality scheme. After the report appeared, it accepted the concept of national standards; it added the controversial five-year/90 percent reduction provisions; and it made use of "handles" to compel industry to comply with the law.

INNOVATIONS IN REGULATORY POLICY

These changes were a major innovation in air pollution policy because they addressed the problem of vague delegation. Similarly the Ash Council staff proposal to create an Environmental Protection Agency was a major innovation. By focusing responsibility in an agency with a comprehensive environmental mission, it addressed arguments made by the critics of regulation that piecemeal development of regulatory programs and the lack of centralized responsibility were reasons for poor regulatory performance. Although neither reform was brought into being by following the rules of classic decision-making, in both instances the actors advanced reasons for the positions they adopted. Senator Muskie and his subcommittee, for instance, had reasons for their insistence on regional as opposed to national air quality standards. They had reasons for favoring health and welfare-based standards as opposed to technologically and economically based standards. They had reasons for wanting to compel technological change and for wanting to force industry to achieve goals by certain dates.

These two case studies in policy choice seem to indicate that an implicit rationality, which strays from decision-making rationality but approximates some of its features, is embedded in the political process. An appropriate conclusion is that actors search for solutions to problems they have to solve until enough of them agree that what they are doing is reasonable. Then they stop searching. As Simon holds, they "satisfice," rather than maximize.

What this familiar argument ignores is that decision-making may take place in entirely separate arenas where different philosophies and approaches to the problem prevail. In this instance problems were defined, but they were defined differently by the White House and Congress. The White House definition was related to the piecemeal development of pollution control programs. Congress' definition was connected to the lack of progress made by the programs for which it was responsible. Within each branch some agreement was reached about goals, but the agreement that each branch reached was different. For the White House, the objective was managing the environment comprehensively and achieving efficiency in making pollution reductions. For Congress, the goal was to make rapid progress with respect to specific pollution control problems. Comprehensive environmental management as envisioned by the White House was not matched by a comprehensive environmental law in Congress that would have given the bureaucracy authority to follow systematically the flow of pollutants and to choose on this basis the most efficient strategy to control pollution.

The proceedings of the White House occurred behind closed doors without the glare of media publicity, while the proceedings of the Muskie subcommittee were affected by negative media attention. In the White House, the policy initially proposed was toned down and idealistic inclinations were tempered. In Congress, on the other hand, caution gave way to intemperance. A modest proposal became a more radical departure.

Notes

1. Accounts of the passage of the 1970 Clean Air Act can be found in the following sources: Charles O. Jones, *Clean Air: The Policies and Politics of Pollution Control* (Pittsburgh: University of Pittsburgh Press, 1975), pp. 175-210; Elia Zuckerman, "Senator Muskie and the 1970 Amendments to the Clean Air Act" (Cambridge, Mass., John F. Kennedy School of Government, 1976); J. Clarence Davies and Barbara Davies, *The Politics of Pollution* (Indianapolis: Bobbs-Merrill, 1975), pp. 52-56; and Henry D. Jacoby, John D. Steinbruner, et al., *Clearing the Air: Federal Policy on Automotive Emissions Control* (Cambridge, Mass.: Ballinger, 1973), pp. 9-15. Comparable accounts of the origin of regulatory legislation can be found in Mark V. Nadel, *The Politics of Consumer Protection* (Indianapolis: Bobbs-Merrill, 1971), pp. 101-55; James E. Anderson, ed., *Politics and Economic Policy-Making* (Reading, Mass.: Addison Wesley, 1970); and David F. Paulsen and Robert B. Denhardt, eds., *Pollution and Public Policy* (New York: Dodd, Mead and Co., 1973). See, for instance, William Letwin, "Congress Passes the Sherman Act," pp. 201-04, and Irving Bernstein, "Congress Passes the Wagner Act," pp. 335-50, in Anderson, *Politics and Economic Policy-Making*, and Randall B. Ripley, "Congress and Clean Air," pp. 175-201, in Paulsen and Denhardt.

2. See Senate Public Works Committee, *Air Pollution Hearings: 1969-70* (Washington, D.C.: U.S. Government Printing Office, 1970).
3. John C. Esposito, *Vanishing Air* (New York: Grossman Publishers, 1970). Charles McCarry has written a lively biography of Nader. See *Citizen Nader* (New York: Saturday Review Press, 1972). Chapter 2 ("Audacity— Always Audacity") of McCarry's biography puts the publication of *Vanishing Air* into the context of Nader's career.
4. The book cover of *Vanishing Air* proclaims "Senator Muskie's sub-committee on pollution and the federal laws for which it is responsible have resulted in a 'business as usual' license to pollute for countless companies across the country."
5. "Such strong criticism of a potential presidential candidate is natu-rally excellent copy for the media, and the newspapers in particular gave the Nader report complete coverage." See Jones, *Clean Air*, p. 192. *The New York Times* published an editorial supporting Muskie and urged closer cooperation between Nader and the senator. Nader used the editorial as an occasion to write a letter to the editor. He defended the report by saying:

At issue is the very integrity of the legal process, presently twisted in the mess of unworkable legislation devoid of the most minimally effective sanctions and riddled with industrial opportunities for endless delay, obfuscation, and attrition of a semistarved federal pollution agency. The chief architect and booster of these laws is Senator Muskie. See Zuckerman, "Senator Muskie and the 1970 Amendments," pp. 4-5.

6. See Zuckerman, "Senator Muskie and the 1970 Amendments," p. 4.
7. Jones, *Clean Air*, p. 192. Steinbruner writes, "The attack by Nader's study group stung Muskie, then a presidential hopeful. It threatened him in an area where he had established a strong public reputation and caught him at a time when he was being pressured from several sides" *Clearing the Air*, p. 11.
8. Davies and Davies, *The Politics of Pollution*, p. 182.
9. Davies and Davies write, "one of Ralph Nader's task forces had published a report on air pollution which called into question Muskie's entire record in pollution legislation....Stung by these criticisms and spurred by the existing pressures, the Muskie subcommittee drafted a bill which far exceeded both the House and administration proposals in strin-gency" (*The Politics of Pollution*, pp. 54-55).
10. James Q. Wilson, "The Politics of Regulation," in *Social Responsibil-ity and the Business Predicament*, ed. James W. McKie (Washington, D.C.: The Brookings Institution, 1974), p. 145.
11. Lazarus writes, "Nader *is* a national scold but this makes him neither unique nor ineffective....The ubiquity and surprising efficacy of shaming in public debate helps to explain why many...causes...attain far greater

political success than the actual power behind them would justify." See Simon Lazarus, *The Genteel Populists* (New York: Holt, Rinehart, and Winston), p. 158.

12. Ibid., p. 79.

13. See Richard C. Leone, "Public Interest Advocacy and the Regulatory Process," in *The Government as Regulator*, ed. Marver H. Bernstein (Philadelphia: The American Academy of Political and Social Science, 1972), p. 55.

14. See Nadel, *The Politics of Consumer Protection*, p. 180.

15. See McCarry, *Citizen Nader*.

16. Ibid.

17. Esposito, *Vanishing Air*, pp. 287-93.

18. See Davies and Davies, *The Politics of Pollution*, pp. 49-52, for a discussion of the 1967 Air Quality Act. Also see John T. Middleton, "Summary of the Air Quality Act of 1967," *Arizona Law Review* (1968) and Sidney Edelman, "Air Pollution Abatement Procedures Under the Clean Air Act," *Arizona Law Review* (1968) reprinted in *Environmental Law and Policy*, ed. James E. Kirier (Indianapolis: Bobbs-Merrill, 1971), pp. 304-07, 321-26.

19. Davies and Davies, *The Politics of Pollution*, p. 182.

20. Clean Air Amendment of 1970, Pub. L. No. 91-604.

21. Esposito, *Vanishing Air*, p. 161, 158.

22. Ibid., p. 274.

23. Ibid., p. 289.

24. Ibid., p. 275.

25. See Jones, *Clean Air*, pp. 176-91.

26. See "The President's Message on the Environment, February 10, 1970," reprinted in Council on Environmental Quality, *Environmental Quality: The First Annual Report* (Washingtion, D.C.: U. S. Government Printing Office, 1970), pp. 260-64. Also see Jones, *Clean Air*, p. 181.

27. Anestis, "A Critical History," in *Environmental Protection*, ed. Louis L. Jaffee and Lawrence H. Tribe (Chicago: The Bracton Press, 1971), pp. 248-49.

20. Robert S. Diamond, "What Business Thinks," *Fortune* (February 1970), p. 119.

29. Esposito, *Vanishing Air*, pp. 5-19.

30. The following sources discuss the harm caused by air pollution: Walsh MacDermott, "Air Pollution and Public Health," reprinted in Ehrlich, Holdren, and Holm, *Man and the Ecosphere: Readings from the Scientific American* (San Francisco: W. H. Freeman, 1971), pp. 137-45; Benjamin G. Ferris, Jr., and James L. Whittenberger, "Effects of Community Air Pollution on Prevalence of Respiratory Disease," reprinted in *Environmental Hazards* (Massachusetts Medical Society, 1966); Lester B. Lave and Eugene P. Seskin, "Air Pollution and Human Health," reprinted in *Economics of the Environment*, ed. Robert Dorfman and Nancy Dorfman (New York: W. W. Norton, 1972), pp. 356-84; Sterling Brubaker, *To Live on Earth* (New York: Mentor, 1972), pp. 149-57; Council on Environmental Quality, *Environmen-*

tal Quality, pp. 62-72; and William Ahern, Jr., "Health Effects of Automotive Pollution," in Jacoby and Steinbruner, *Clearing the Air,* pp. 139-75.

31. See Wilson, "The Politics of Regulation," p. 146.

32. Ibid., p. 152.

33. Lazarus, *The Genteel Populists,* p. 79, and Leone, "Public Interest Advocacy," p. 53.

34. Wilson, *The Politics of Regulation,* p. 143.

35. See Roger Noll, *Reforming Regulation: An Evaluation of the Ash Council Proposals* (Washington, D.C.: The Brookings Institution, 1971).

36. See Theodore Lowi, *The End of Liberalism* (New York: W. W. Norton, 1969), p. 126. Lowi derives this notion about delegation primarily from Kenneth Culp Davis. See Kenneth Culp Davis, *Administrative Law Treatise* (St. Paul: West Publishing Company, 1958), especially pp. 9-53. Also see Kenneth Culp Davis, *Discretionary Justice: A Preliminary Inquiry* (Urbana, Ill. University of Illionois Press, 1977), and Henry J. Friendly, *The Federal Administrative Agencies* (Cambridge, Mass.: Harvard University Press, 1962).

37. See Bernstein, *Regulating Business by Independent Commission,* (Princeton, N.J.: Princeton University Press, 1955), pp. 263-67; Merle Fainsod, "The Nature of the Regulatory Process," in *Public Policy 1940,* ed. C. J. Friedrich and E. S. Mason (Cambridge, Mass.: Harvard University Press, 1940), pp. 297-323; and Samuel P. Huntington, *Clientalism: A Study in Administrative Politics* (Harvard University Government Department, 1950). For a summary of this literature, see Barry Mitnick, "A Critique of Life Cycle Theories of Regulation," working paper (Ohio State University, College of Administrative Science, 1978).

38. Theodore Lowi, *The End of Liberalism,* pp. 125-56.

39. See Muskie quote in Zuckerman, "Senator Muskie and the 1970 Amendments," pp. 18-19.

40. See Frank P. Grad, Albert Rosenthal, et al., *The Automobile and the Regulation of Its Impact on the Environment* (Norman, Okla.: University of Oklahoma Press, 1975), pp. 325-38. It led to repeated confrontations with the auto manufacturers and to the prospect that the cars produced in the United States in 1978 would be illegal.

41. See Bernard Asbell, "The Outlawing of Next Year's Cars," *The New York Times Magazine* (November 21, 1976), p. 41.

42. See Jacoby and Steinbruner, *Clearing the Air,* pp. 27-47.

43. For a recent discussion of alternatives to the internal combustion engine, see Arnold W. Reitze, Jr., "An Otto for the Automobile," *Environment* (May 1977), pp. 32-42.

44. See Howard Margolis, "The Politics of Auto Emissions," *The Public Interest* (Fall 1977), pp. 3-22.

45. See Jones, *Clean Air,* p. 206.

46. See Muskie quote in Zuckerman, "Senator Muskie and the 1970 Amendments," p. 24.

47. Ibid., p. 245.
48. *Congressional Record* (December 15, 1970), pp. 520597-99.
49. Zuckerman, "Senator Muskie and the 1970 Amendments," p. 28.

PART II

IMPLEMENTATION

3

Receiving Instructions: The Priorities of the New Administrator

Implementation is the receiving and carrying out of instructions. The bureaucracy, the appointed officials and permanent civil servants that EPA inherited, had to receive and carry out the policy instructions that the White House and Congress formulated. William Ruckelshaus, EPA's first administrator, responded to the instructions he received from the White House and Congress by developing three priorities when he took over the agency.[1] He wanted to create a well-defined enforcement image, scrupulously carry out the provisions of the 1970 Clean Air Act, and gain control over the costs of regulatory decision-making. Establishing priorities for the new agency was not a planned and orderly procedure. Ruckelshaus compared it to "running a 100-yard dash, while undergoing an appendectomy."[2]

He coped with issues as they arose and responded to what he considered to be the requirements of the moment. His first priority—to bring significant numbers of pollution control violators to court—was established in response to his perception of what the public wanted. It was influenced only marginally by what officials in the White House and Congress expected. His subsequent priorities—to issue clean air regulations according to the timetables mandated by Congress

and to gain control over the costs of regulatory decisions—
were directly influenced by conflicting White House and congressional pressures. Congress wanted EPA to issue healthy
air regulations according to the timetables it established in
1970. The 1970 Clean Air Act stated explicitly that the
administrator should *not* take costs into account when issuing regulations. The White House, however, applied pressure
to get the agency to consider costs. Its primary concern was
not that the 1975 healthy air goal be achieved but that the
economic implications of pollution control decisions be carefully examined. Ruckelshaus developed priorities in response
to these opposing pressures. How he coped with his initial
freedom from close supervision and how he managed the
contradictory pressures the two branches subsequently applied will be the subject of this chapter.

The First Priority: Enforcement and Image Building

When President Nixon chose William Ruckelshaus, a relatively obscure Justice Department attorney, to be EPA's first
administrator, Ruckelshaus' experience in the environmental field was limited.[3] In the early 1960s, working out of the
Indiana attorney general's office, he helped draft the state's
air pollution abatement actions, but since that time—as state
legislator, Senate candidate, and Justice Department official
under John Mitchell—he had had no involvement in environmental affairs. When his selection was made public, an
Indiana conservationist called him "an environmental
Carswell"—a nominee with no credentials.[4]

Excited about the prospect of being the "founding father"
of a new agency and concerned about people's mistrust of
government institutions, Ruchelshaus' immediate goal was
to help to restore public confidence in government.[5] He
believed that he should represent the average citizen who
saw pollution all around him, who knew that there were laws
on the books, and who wondered why the government was
not doing anything about it.

On the day of his selection, Ruckelshaus was briefed first by President Nixon and then by John Whitaker, the Domestic Council official who was an aide to John Erlichman. The president gave the impression that he considered the environmental problem faddish. Whitaker said that Erlichman cared about the organizational aspects of the problem, and that Fred Malek's executive search group within the Domestic Council was likely to keep close tabs on Ruckelshaus' appointments. The other executive office with which EPA would have to deal—the Council on Environmental Quality— was sympathetic to the agency.

After Ruckelshaus communicated with the White House, he met with environmental and industrial lobbyists. The lobbyists tried to "feel him out." The environmental spokespersons showed some apprehension that a "Mitchell confidant" was heading EPA, but their attitude was to wait until Ruckelshaus demonstrated his preferences before judging him. At a meeting with industrial leaders, convened by a congressional Republican Club, Ruckelshaus was also treated as if he were an unknown quantity by the industrial lobbyists who were present.

At the nomination hearings, which received television coverage, members of the Senate pollution control subcommittee lectured Ruckelshaus about vested interests that were endangering the public health and public agencies that were not showing enough zeal in going after pollutors.[6] Although members of the pollution control subcommittee supported vigorous enforcement by EPA, the new administrator realized that fifteen other congressional subcommittees with diverse attitudes had some jurisdiction over EPA's pollution control activities. The most prominent of these was the House Appropriations Subcommittee on Agriculture, Environment, and Consumer Protection, headed by Jamie Whitten (D.—Miss.). In contrast to Muskie, Whitten was a conservative on environmental protection issues. For years he had fought Rachel Carson and opposed pesticide regulation. Ruckelshaus believed that generous authorizations made by Muskie's subcommittee would be converted into miserly appropriations if Whitten's influence were not neutralized by consistent public pressure for a strong environmental policy.

In the period immediately following EPA's creation, the bureaucracy that the agency inherited was disorganized.[7] It had no central location. (It did not move into its present headquarters at Waterside Mall until 1973.) Programming, planning and evaluation, and management information systems were not in operation. Also, no standard accounting system existed to allocate funds. Without standard management systems, communication betwen EPA offices scattered throughout Washington was a problem. The agency did not have a single identity.

The reorganization existed on paper only. Since the reorganization order did not always specify exactly what was to be transferred to EPA, the new agency was involved in lengthy negotiations to secure some of its components. HEW proved particularly reluctant to relinquish some of the scientists and laboratories that had been promised. In this transition period EPA employees still sat at their desks in their old offices generally doing the same things they had been doing before EPA was created.

Ruckelshaus was accustomed to operations in which attorneys brought violators of federal law to court for prosecution. To undertake a suit strategy, Ruckelshaus could rely on the legal staff that he brought into the agency with him. From the bureaucracy all he needed was advice about appropriate targets.

Ruckelshaus' first priority as administrator was to try to build the reputation of the new agency as a vigorous enforcer of pollution control laws. The agencies EPA inherited were known for their research. Capable of "studying a problem to death," they had not shown an ability to take decisive action against known violators of pollution control laws. When EPA was created Ruckelshaus tried to reverse this image by means of an activist suit strategy.

In the first week of EPA's existence, Ruckelshaus sued major municipal and industrial pollutors.[8] He took Atlanta,

Detroit, and Cleveland to court for sewage waste discharges in violation of the 1965 Water Quality Act. To attract media attention he made the announcement on December 10, 1970, at the National League of Cities convention in Atlanta. On December 17, the agency asked the Justice Department to prosecute Jones and Laughlin Steel for discharging pollutants into the Cayohoga River near Cleveland and U.S. Plywood-Champion Paper for polluting the Ohio River. In the same month it reconvened a Lake Superior enforcement conference dealing with Reserve Mining's taconite wastes. By February it had initiated suits against ARMCO Steel for its discharges into the Houston ship channel and ITT-Rayonier for its pulp mill operations on Puget Sound. U.S. Steel, Union Carbide, du Pont, and General Motors also were brought to court for pollution control violations. In its first two months, EPA brought five times as many enforcement actions as all of the agencies it inherited had initiated in any previous two-month period.[9]

The suit strategy, which only required the involvement of the attorneys Ruckelshaus brought into the agency, established credibility with the concerned public. Ruckelshaus received publicity and attention. He gave frequent interviews to the press, appeared on television talk shows, and spoke often in front of municipal and business organizations.

John Quarles, first assistant administrator for enforcement at EPA, explains Ruckelshaus' first priority:

Ruckelshaus believed in the strength of public opinion and public support. The organized environmental movement had been formed because of public pressure and Ruckelshaus responded instinctively to that pressure. He did not seek support for his actions in the established structures of political power. He turned instead directly to the press and to public opinion, often in conflict with those very structures. In so doing, he tied the fortunes of EPA to public opinion as the only base for political support.[10]

Ruckelshaus was worried about the environmentalists' tendency to represent public officials as either friends or enemies of the pollutors. By questioning the agency's willingness to prosecute he feared that they could undermine public confidence in EPA. In order to establish credibility with environmental groups, Ruckelshaus believed that the agency had to cultivate an "activist image" and had to acquire the reputation of being a vigorous enforcer of pollution control laws.

The Second Priority: Meeting Statutory Deadlines

Ruckelshaus' second priority—meeting statutory deadlines—was imposed by the requirements of the Clean Air Act.[11] Thirty days after the enactment of the 1970 Clean Air Act, the administrator had to propose national ambient air quality standards that would commit the agency to health and welfare goals that it had to meet according to a congressionally mandated timetable.

Officials from the old National Air Pollution Control Administration (NAPCA) that EPA inherited from the Department of Health, Education, and Welfare assumed responsibility for setting these air quality goals. Using scientific evidence and the judgments that they had formed about the effects of air pollutants on public health and welfare, they drafted a full set of standards and presented them to Ruckelshaus three days before the statutory deadline. Former NAPCA Commissioner John Middelton, who gave the standards to Ruckelshaus, told him that every scientist who had looked at the problem during the last decade agreed with the figures NAPCA was proposing. Members of the Senate and the House accepted these figures, and Congress passed the Clean Air Act with them in mind.

Ruckelshaus had three days to review the standards. He found it difficult in such a short period of time to evaluate them. He had not inherited a bureaucratic unit that could do an independent analysis, and he felt that because of the time constraints that Congress wrote into the 1970 Clean Air Act he had no choice but to accept the standards that NAPCA officials gave him.

Curious about how someone with a scientific background would view the standards, Ruckelshaus gave them to Stanley Greenfield, his newly appointed scientific advisor. Greenfield, a former Rand Corporation analyst (who later was appointed EPA's assistant administrator for research and development) was critical of standards he considered overly stringent and basically unachievable. Greenfield thought that there were problems with the use of the data and scientific information to support the standards. He maintained that other options should have been considered because the evidence that NAPCA presented was open to different interpretations.

Ruckelshaus did not have the time or ability to asses Greenfield's objections. He felt that he had to announce the new air quality standards in accord with the statutory timetable. At the news conference at which Ruckelshaus and newly appointed Assistant Administrator for Enforcement John Quarles announced the standards, they had to have cue cards on which the names of the pollutants for which they were issuing regulations were written. They had not grappled with the implications of the standards and were uncertain if the agency could actually achieve them.

Some of the standards, as Greenfield suggested, were immediately challenged in the courts. The Kennecott Copper Corporation, for instance, challenged one of the sulfur dioxide standards. It claimed that there was no adequate scientific evidence to support this standard, and the court remanded it to EPA for further consideration.

Very dissatisfied with the experience of issuing regulations without adequate preparation or analysis and with the subsequent court challenges, Ruckelshaus began to look more closely at the other regulatory deadlines in the 1970 Clean Air Act. EPA had a series of relatively long-term deadlines, such as those relating to motor vehicles, where it had to make sure that the auto companies reduced carbon monoxide and hydrocarbon emissions 90 percent by 1975 and nitrogen oxides emissions 90 percent by 1976. It also had a series of relatively short-term deadlines where it had to make sure

TABLE 9
Deadlines in the 1970 Clean Air Act

Major Goal	Timetable
Air suitable for human health	Quality standards proposed January 31, 1971, and promulgated April 30, 1971.

Means

1. 90 percent reduction in auto exhaust	HC and CO reductions have to be achieved by 1975; NO_x reductions by 1976
2. State implementation plans:	States must submit plans by January 30, 1972; reviewed and promulgated by EPA June 30, 1972
a. Stationary source emmission standards b. Transportation control plans if necessary	State plans have to achieve minimum health level for major pollutants by July 30, 1975

that states issued implementation plans in accord with congressional deadlines. Nine months after the promulgation of the national air quality standards, each state had to adopt an implementation plan. The state had to relate emission production from industrial sources to ambient air quality goals and develop a "roll back technique" which would involve a percentage reduction on the part of major emitters. The purpose of these plans was to achieve healthy air by 1975. After each state wrote its plan, EPA had to review it. If the state submitted a plan that EPA found unacceptable, the agency had the right to impose a different plan. If necessary

EPA could make use of transportation control measures in the revised plan to achieve healthy air by 1975.

After reviewing the regulations EPA had to issue under the Clean Air Act, Ruckelshaus became aware that EPA had received very explicit instructions from Congress that gave it very little leeway. If he was to maintain satisfactory relations with Congress, the administrator could not devote himself only to litigation. He had to meet congressionally mandated deadlines.

Once he became more aware of the full extent of the congressional requirements, Ruckelshaus privately, not publicly, became more critical of the requirements of the Clean Air Act. He believed that the auto emissions limitations were too stringent, that the 1975 and 1976 deadlines were too short a time for a technical problem that had no easy solution. In addition, he felt that the air quality goals he had already promulgated asked for too much reduction from the states and would either discourage the state authorities from issuing the state implementation plans at all or lead them to promulgate plans that they did not intend to enforce. Finally, Ruckelshaus had questions about the appropriateness of the transportation control measure that the agency might have to use under the 1970 statute.

Even though he privately had these reservations about the law he was required to implement, he felt that to maintain EPA's credibility with Congress, he needed to make a "good faith" effort to carry out what Congress intended. Ruckelshaus believed that the deadlines in the 1970 Clean Air Act expressed Congress' growing mistrust of the bureaucracy. Congress was displeased with NAPCA's poor performance in implementing the 1967 Air Quality Act. The deadlines and the carefully organized steps to reach air quality goals that had been put in the new statute were designed to force progress from EPA and industry. Ruckelshaus concluded that because of the antibureaucratic mood among congressmen the agency had to meet the deadlines and carry out the provisions of the Clean Air Act as Congress intended.

Ruckelshaus believed that EPA could go to Congress to change the statute only after it had made every effort to carry out the act as it was written. The administrator could not ask Congress to change the statute unless he could show specific instances where the act had not been effective. By making a "good faith" effort to implement the statute, EPA could convince Congress that parts of the act had to be revised. The agency therefore had to prod the states into coming up with the implementation plans, rewrite the state plans when they proved inadequate, and adopt changes when necessary to show Congress that there were deficiencies in the way it had drafted the act.

Ruckelshaus was committed to meeting the deadlines in the Clean Air Act because he feared the power of Muskie's subcommittee. Muskie's pollution control subcommittee had broad oversight responsibilities over EPA. It controlled authorizations for air and water pollution and was led by an aspiring presidential candidate, who at the time was determined to keep environmental issues at the center of national attention. Ruckelshaus repeatedly appeared before Muskie's subcommittee and heard criticism from the senator when he believed that EPA was showing signs of weakness. Ruckelshaus considered Muskie and his subcommittee formidable watchdogs of EPA behavior and felt that it was important to satisfy them by carefully carrying out the 1970 Clean Air Act as Congress intended. Ruckelshaus' unpreparedness when promulgating air quality goals and the scrutiny to which Congress subjected him were reasons he made meeting statutory deadlines his second priority.

The Third Priority: Control

Ruckelshaus' third priority was to gain some control over the regulatory decision-making process.[12] This priority was both a response to the lack of preparedness he experienced when he approved the air quality goals and a response to White House pressures that Ruckelshaus take into account the economic implications of EPA's regulatory decisions. After he made the decision to accept air quality goals, Ruckelshaus was convinced that the agency needed bureaucrats who were not associated with the inherited civil service to review future standards and assess options. However, he only took steps to bring in new officials to carry out this function in the summer of 1971 when the White House started what has been referred to as an "ecological backlash."

The president sided with those who wanted to eliminate the worst hazards from the air and water, but he made it abundantly clear that his first priority was economic progress. He often expressed the opinion that the environmental problem was transitory, would not be prominent for long, and that the main responsibility of the government was to insure continued economic growth and prosperity and not to improve environmental quality. The president's attitude was reflected by his aides who made Ruckelshaus feel anxious about the independent constituency he was creating among environmentalists. They made him feel as if the measure of success for a Nixon appointee was loyalty and that by this measure he was not succeeding.

Some of the White House staff made efforts to intervene in regulatory decision-making. For example when Peter Flanigan, a member of the White House staff, received a call from ARMCO Steel protesting that EPA was trying to shut down its plant in Dallas, Flanigan summoned EPA's Assistant Administrator for Enforcement John Quarles to his office. Quarles related what happened:

On Wednesday morning, September 29, 1971, I received a hurried request to come to the office of Peter Flanigan in the White House early that afternoon. I had seen Flanigan before only once or twice, and did not know him personally, but his reputation marked him as a potentionally dangerous critic of EPA. Flanigan had come to the White House from Wall Street and had brought with him the belief that the business of American is business.... Flanigan turned to a letter he had just received from William Verity, president of ARMCO Steel. Verity was not only a powerful figure in American industry; but I had also heard that he was a well-known and influential leader in the Ohio Republican party.
Flanigan argued that our action [against ARMCO] was inconsistent with the president's policy and that it was up to EPA to conform.[13]

Quarles tried to assure Flanigan that EPA was not trying to shut down the ARMCO plant in question, but that it was trying to get the company to agree to a compliance schedule. However Quarles' efforts with Flanigan were unsuccessful. Flanigan continued to apply pressure. After an article in a Washington newspaper revealed that the White House had intervened on behalf of a company whose officers and directors had contributed to Nixon's 1968 presidential campaign, Flanigan stopped pressuring the agency.

Nixon's attitude and these run-ins with White House officials chipped away at EPA's authority. Ruckelshaus felt that he had to do something to show the White House that the agency was concerned about economic impact. Instead of emphasizing image-building activities and environmental enforcement as he would have preferred, he had to contend with the demands made by the White House that EPA take into account the economic impact of its regulatory decisions. Ruckelshaus felt that a mechanism for regulatory review was needed to satisfy the White House. The civil servants EPA inherited had a scientific point of view that excluded weighing costs and benefits. They were supported by Congress. The administrator, however, to satisfy the White House needed to establish a means to review the work of the bureaucracy in an effort to check it for economic implications.

To insure control over regulatory decision-making, Ruckelshaus asked Robert Sansom—an economist who had been on Henry Kissinger's National Security Council staff— to join EPA. Sansom would be the head of a steering committee that would review and evaluate proposed standards and regulations. The steering committee process was supposed to work in the following fashion.[14] The old program offices, which had the bulk of experienced personnel and were capable of responding immediately to the deadlines in EPA's legislation, were supposed to take the lead in the regulatory process. The original data collection and analysis would be done by them and they would make a recommendation to the steering committee. The steering committee then would review this analysis and make efforts to improve it. It would bring together officials from other EPA offices to see what problems and weaknesses were involved and to provide a clearer understanding of the regulation's ramifications. Lawyers from the Office of Enforcement would check legal implications, scientists from the Office of Research and Development would check scientific implications, and economists working under Sansom would make a final tally of costs and benefits.

One of the purposes of this decision-making process was to bring agency differences of opinion out into the open. If agreement was impossible, the administrator would be given a number of options and the evidence needed to weigh the pros and cons of the options. If there were two or three ways of addressing a particular problem, he could pick the least costly alternative. By generating options, this process was supposed to give the administrator the control he needed over regulatory decision-making.

Summary

Although designed to please the White House, the use of the steering committee review process went against the spirit of what Congress intended. In passing the 1970 Clean Air Act Congress explicitly stated that EPA should issue regulations without regard to their economic implications. Congress wanted deadlines met and progress achieved by certain dates without lengthy analyses and discussion of regulatory costs. According to the statute it passed, improving public health and not economic impact was the primary consideration.

Although initially free to pursue an enforcement strategy that pleased him because of his professional background and personal values, Ruckelshaus ultimately became caught in the middle of this struggle between the White House and Congress over how the 1970 Clean Air Act was to be interpreted and implemented. He established priorities designed to please each branch, but he could not satisfy either branch entirely because what he did to please Congress (promptly meet statutory deadlines) incurred the disfavor of the White House since promptly meeting deadlines did not take into account economic impact.

In conceiving EPA's priorities Ruckelshaus responded to these contradictory pressures. The extent to which he could exhibit discretion therefore was limited. Concerned about declining public confidence in the government, he pursued pollutors and tried to achieve public recognition as a vigorous prosecutor of pollution control offenders. His legal background influenced his decision to prepare cases against violators and prejudiced him against a management solution to EPA's problems. For the most part he ignored EPA's organizational disarray and relied on the attorneys he brought to the agency. The suit strategy built an image of vigor and integrity in the media and won public acclaim, but the extent to which he could carry it out was limited. Statutory responsibilities and White House pressures started to influence his activities directly. To satisfy a potentially critical Congress, Ruckelshaus tried to execute scrupulously a law whose ultimate feasibility he doubted. To show loyalty to a president who was anxious about the economic impact of pollution regulation, he tried to establish a decision-making procedure that would balance environmental benefits and economic costs.

The agency's priorities represented "some sort of conjunction" of the goals of the members of a "coalition" that included the White House, Congress, environmentalists, and public opinion.[15] The priorities of this coalition changed depending upon which members of the coalition were active at a particular moment. When Congress and the White House were inactive, the administrator had discretion to follow the lead of environmentalists and public opinion. When the two branches were active, his discretion was checked by the contradictory pressures they applied.

This outcome, where in effect Ruckelshaus became a "broker" making temporary adjustments among competing interests and institutions, may not be different from what regulatory reformers intended when they called for the creation of agencies with single administrators chosen by the president and for explicit statutory provisions enacted by Congress. These reforms were designed to make agencies accountable to the executive and the legislature. Under these conditions an administrator becomes a broker who has to maintain a "working balance" between competing interests and values.[16] His power is "important but limited."[17] He is a tactician who must "yield here, stand firm there, delay at the next point, and again act vigorously in a confusing complex of competing forces and interests."[18] His tactical maneuvers are a sign of his independence. Wholly endorsed by no one, the broker is "subject to the criticism of all."[19]

Notes

1. The literature on executive behavior includes the following: Chester I. Barnard, *The Functions of the Executive* (Cambridge, Mass.: Harvard University Press, 1938, 1968); Phillip Selznick, *Leadership in Administration* (New York: Harper & Row, 1957); Marver Bernstein, *The Job of the Federal Executive* (Washington, D.C.: Brookings Institution, 1958) and Harold Seidman, *Politics, Position and Power* (New York: Oxford University Press, 1970).

2. John Quarles, *Cleaning Up America* (Boston: Houghton Mifflin, 1976), p. 32.

3. On Ruckelshaus' background and his appointment, see Quarles, *Cleaning Up America*, pp. 14-36. Also see Richard Corrigan, "Environment Report/Success of New Agency Depends Upon Ruckelshaus Direction," *National Journal Report* (December 19, 1970), pp. 2591-95; and Gregory Mills, "William Ruckelshaus and the EPA" (Cambridge, Mass.: John F. Kennedy School of Government, 1974).

4. Mills, "William Ruckelshaus and the EPA," p. 5.

5. See Peggy Wiehl, "William D. Ruckelshaus and the Environmental Protection Agency" (Cambridge, Mass.: John F. Kennedy School of Government, 1974), p. 3.

6. Senate Public Works Committee, *Nomination of William D. Ruckelshaus Hearings* (December 1, 2, 1970).

7. See William R. Ahern, Jr., "Organizing for Pollution Control: The Beginnings of the Environmental Protection Agency, 1970-1971" (Cambridge, Mass.: John F. Kennedy School of Government, 1973); also see Robert Gillette, "Environmental Protection Agency: Chaos or 'Creative Tension'?", *Science* (August 20, 1971), pp. 703-07.

8. See Quarles, *Cleaning Up America*, pp. 37-58 and Wiehl, "William D. Ruckelshaus," pp. 8-13.

9. U.S. EPA, *The First Two Years: A Review of EPA's Enforcement Program* (February 1973).

10. Quarles, *Cleaning Up America*, p. 36.

11. See *The Clean Air Amendments of 1970—P.L. 91-604* (December 31, 1970); also see Stevens, "Air Pollution and the Federal System: Responses to Felt Necessities," in *Environmental Law and Policy*, ed. James Krier (Indianapolis: Bobbs-Merrill, 1971), pp. 351-53.

12. The problem of control is discussed in Anthony Downs, *Inside Bureaucracy* (Boston, Mass.: Little, Brown and Co., 1967), and Herbert Kaufman, *Administrative Feedback* (Washington, D.C.: The Brookings Institution, 1973).

13. Quarles, *Cleaning Up America*, pp. 61-64.

14. Codified in December 1971 under the title of EPA Order 1000.6. On December 6, 1974, EPA's second administrator, Russell E. Train, issued a "Standards and Regulations Manual" which codified Order 1000.6 and revised its procedures. The purposes of the manual included broader participation, improved clarity, considering alternative approaches, and energy analysis. See U.S. EPA, "Procedures For the Standards and Regulations Development Process" (Office of Planning and Management, December 6, 1974); also see "Proposed Environmental Protection Agency Consumer Representation Plan" (October 31, 1975).

15. See Joseph L. Bower, "Descriptive Decision Theory from the Administrative Viewpoint," in *The Study of Policy Formation*, ed. Raymond A Bauer and Kenneth J. Gergen (New York: The Free Press, 1968), pp. 129-38.

16. See V. O. Key, *Politics, Parties and Pressure Groups* (New York: T. Y. Crowell Co., 1942).

17. Quarles, *Cleaning Up America*, p. 169.

18. Key, *Politics, Parties and Pressure Groups*, pp. 23-24.

19. Ibid.

4

Receiving Instructions: A Divided Bureaucracy

The agency that Ruckelshaus headed was structured in such a way that it was supposed to serve two masters; it served neither faithfully. EPA was not a single organism with a single will but a series of different organisms with different wills. It lacked unity and without unity it had difficulty fulfilling the intentions of either the White House or Congress.

The conflict between the intentions of the White House and Congress became embedded in EPA's structure. Some of the agency's offices essentially served the White House, some essentially served Congress, and some had the freedom to pursue their own objectives without contributing to the achievement of White House or congressional goals. The bureaucrats that served the White House tried to adjust the agency to changing priorities, to the shift from an environmental focus to a concern about the economy and the adequacy of the nation's energy supply. Those that served Congress tried to achieve statutory objectives. Those that were removed from the conflict between presidential and congressional ambitions were research scientists. They had a professional orientation and a long-term time perspective that had little bearing on the realization of the goals of the President or Congress.

How the Conflict between White House and Congressional Intentions Became Embedded in EPA's Structure

EPA was partially organized to carry out presidential wishes. The president's message that accompanied the reorganization order that created the EPA stressed the notion of comprehensive environmental management. Such a concept meant eliminating the separate treatment accorded to different forms of pollution. A plan to organize EPA to manage the environment as a whole was formulated in the period before the agency started operations.[1]

In this period, Alain Enthoven, who was a White House consultant, helped devise an organizational strategy.[2] Enthoven, a former Defense Department official, composed a functional plan that was introduced on October 5, 1970, about two months before EPA started operations. Enthoven's plan incorporated ideas that the Ash Council staff had been developing and ideas that appealed to Enthoven because they applied Defense Department program planning experiments to EPA's organizational design.[3] Just as Defense Department budget categories were divided into functional units (such as strategic retaliation, general purpose, air defense), so EPA's organizational division could be divided into functional units (such as abatement, monitoring, research, standard setting). Just as Defense Department mission-based categories were supposed to eliminate artificial bureaucratic distinctions, reduce duplication and waste, and achieve greater integration of operations, so EPA mission-based divisions were supposed to do away with archaic bureaucratic distinctions, promote cost-effectiveness, and achieve greater coordination.

In the plan for the functional management that Enthoven composed, he argued forcefully for eliminating EPA's programmatic inheritance: its distinct and separate air pollution, water quality, solid waste, radiation, and pesticide control elements. EPA, according to Enthoven, should carry out President Nixon's expressed intent and deal with the environment as an interrelated system. Abatement programs had to be evaluated on the basis of their total effect on the environment, not on the basis of their effects on a single medium, such as the air, water, or land.

Douglas Costle, a member of the Ash Council's environmental protection group, directed the White House task force that handled transitional issues in the period between congressional approval of the reorganization and the actual start of EPA's operations.[4] He had to decide whether to recommend Enthoven's proposal to Ruckelshaus. Costle was convinced that EPA's bureaucratic sections needed to be molded into an agency with a comprehensive pollution control identity. EPA could not afford to become a big holding company, like the departments of Health, Education, and Welfare or Interior, where the secretaries had little power over intact units with independent constituencies and congressional relations. In Costle's judgment, EPA needed strong management from the top as in the Department of Defense, NASA, and the Atomic Energy Commission.

However, in choosing an organizational strategy Costle balanced the need for hierarchy and integration with the need to "hit the ground running." He feared that if the new administrator would take apart and reassign personnel by function, he would create chaos. Work would come to a halt, and the ensuing confusion would paralyze the agency's efforts. If the full functional scheme were put into effect, the agency would not be able to deal with pressing statutory responsibilities. It would draw criticism from Congress and would be politically vulnerable from attack by public interest activists.

The managers of EPA's sections would not go along with a fully functional, integrated plan. Most of their programs came from large departments (HEW, Interior, and Agriculture) where they enjoyed substantial autonomy. They preferred the holding company model with five self-contained parts (air, water, pesticides, radiation and noise, and solid wastes), each having substantial autonomy. If the old pattern with program managers directing intact units were eliminated, Costle reasoned that there would be disruption of ordinary work routines and bureaucratic opposition.

Costle came to the conclusion that although a functional organization was the appropriate long-term goal for the agency, an incremental organization strategy was reasonable and feasible in the short-term.[5] The message he conveyed to Ruckelshaus at an initial briefing on organization and management options was the EPA should start by maintaining substantial continuity with its programmatic past. The administrator should lay the groundwork for a fully integrated scheme, but he should not start by attempting to eliminate program distinctions entirely. In the short-term, program identity was necessary to carry out statutory requirements. In a follow-up period, Ruckelshaus would be able to overcome the limitations of the holding company pattern.

Costle recommended that initially the five program areas should be preserved: air, water, pesticides, solid waste, and radiation and noise. After a period of time elapsed, three new assistant administrator offices (for Planning and Management, Standards and Compliance, and Research and Monitoring) should be created, but the individual programs should be allowed to retain their separate identities in the remaining assistant administrator offices. Only after more time had elapsed, should Ruckelshaus eliminate the program distinctions entirely.

Ruckelshaus, while making slight modifications, essentially carried out the first two stages of Costle's plan. At the start of his tenure, he set up a commissioner system with separate commissioners responsible for the five different programs. In a letter to the agency on the day of his swearing-in, he told his new employees that for the time being he wanted them to "keep moving ahead with the valuable work under way," but ultimately he would work with them to build a new and "effective" organization. Ruckelshaus implied that the commissioner system would be temporary.

Five months later, in April 1971, Ruckelshaus drew up a second organizational plan. This structure basically corresponded to the second stage envisioned by Costle. While Ruckelshaus carried out the first two stages of the plan, neither he nor subsequent administrators pushed the agency to stage three and complete integration. Program offices have survived and maintained their identities. Integration was not completed for a number of reasons. To begin with, Ruckelshaus shied away from it because of his feeling that structure was not that important.[6] Working all his life with lawyers in collegial surroundings, he had no experience as a manager of a hierarchical agency. He did not feel he fully understood the significance of the jargon his organizational advisors used and the meaning of the charts they brought to him. Rather than emphasizing integration of the agency's structure, he focused on getting key people in important positions.[7]

In addition, Ruckelshaus feared a lack of cooperation on the part of the inherited bureaucracy. He did not believe that the

TABLE 10
Ruckelshaus' Second Organizational Plan

Administrator Deputy Administrator	Staff Offices Legislation Equal Opportunity International Affairs Public Affairs

Asst. Admin. for Planning & Management (Noise)	Asst. Admin. for Enforcement & General Counsel	Asst. Admin. for Media Programs	Asst. Admin. for Categorical Programs (Pesticides, Radiation & Solid Wastes)	Asst. Admin. for Research & Monitoring

inherited personnel would accept integrated management. Program managers were linked to specific statutes and principles and were unable to view the environment as a single interrelated system. Many of the program managers had worked in their particular pollution control fields for twenty years or more and had developed very particular expertises. They had carved out specific niches and areas of interest. They were not about to make major changes in existing policy and procedure just because of the administrator's suggestions. They were used to the way decisions had been made and operations carried out, and they believed that the established methods incorporated the lessons of experience.

If Ruckelshaus had imposed the integrated model, morale would have suffered and the agency might have been paralyzed. The inherited bureaucrats would have complained to Congress, where their complaining would have been well-received. Senators and representatives also would have been confused by an organizational structure that eliminated the familiar programmatic categories. To avoid the prospect of an uncooperative bureaucracy and the possibility of congressional criticism, Ruckelshaus decided to maintain a degree of program continuity.

One of the remarkable features about the partially integrated/partially programmatic structure that Ruckelshaus adopted was the amount of discord it brought into being.[8] The division of assistant administrator offices—between integrated offices oriented toward presidential objectives and programmatic offices toward congressional objectives—contributed to in-fighting and competitiveness. It can be argued that the agency was in need of "creative tension" so that it could react promptly to rapidly changing perceptions of the environmental problems. However, it also can be argued that the competitive situation resulted in unnecessary and counterproductive conflict between agency offices. Because of the partially integrated/partially programmatic scheme, no office was certain where its responsibilities might bring it into conflict with other offices.

The Situation and Task of Bureaucrats

The bureaucrats who served EPA had different perspectives depending on the positions they occupied and the tasks they performed.[9] They can be divided into three groups: (1) those with a policy perspective; (2) those with a program perspective; and (3) those with a research perspective. This section will describe the differences among bureaucrats with these perspectives.[10]

THE POLICY PERSPECTIVE

Those with a policy perspective felt that they had to defend the agency against the charges that its actions were contributing to unemployment, inflation, and energy dependence. They were accountable to the national policy concerns that were of importance to the White House. The White House was concerned about the conflict between environmental objectives and other national priorities. Those who had a policy perspective reflected White House thinking within the agency and provided the evidence and arguments EPA needed to justify its decisions when challenged by the White House. They did economic determinations and, after the oil embargo, energy-related studies.

Robert Sansom, the head of the steering committee, was an EPA bureaucrat with a policy perspective. He tried to get program managers to examine the effect of individual regulations on specific industries and the entire economy. His job was to make sure that good economic analysis was done and that a proper balance was reached between environmental and economic objectives. Others performed a similar function with respect to energy. Those with a policy perspective were found mostly in the Office of Planning and Management, not among the mass of accountants and management system analysts that this office employed, but in a few specialized jobs in deputy assistant administrator offices, such as the Office of Policy and Evaluation that employed Sansom. Those with a policy perspective criticized proposed decisions from within the agency, but once these decisions were made, they provided the evidence and arguments needed to defend the agency from criticism from without.

THE PROGRAM PERSPECTIVE

Most bureaucrats had a program perspective rather than a policy perspective. The great bulk of bureaucrats were program managers and operators. They were tied to specific laws, functions, and appropriations. They took their cues from Congress and reflected the fragmented nature of the legislative branch which passed separate pollution control laws and amended them according to different principles.[11]

Pollution control programs had different origins. Federal water legislation goes back to the nineteenth century when Congress enacted a Rivers and Harbor Act.[12] The federal government's concern with air pollution began only in 1955 with an act that authorized federally funded research. In the 1960s the separate development of pollution control programs continued. New water quality, motor vehicle emissions, and air quality acts were passed: the 1965 Water Quality Act provided for the setting of state water quality standards; the 1965 Motor Vehicle Act provided for the setting of national motor vehicle emissions standards; and the 1967 Air Quality Act adopted a regional approach to air quality.[13] Both the motor vehicle and air quality acts were amended by the 1970 Clean Air Act (discussed in Chapter 2).[14] The environmental concerns of the 1960s—water pollution and air pollution—were covered by acts with different provisions and different histories of amendment.

The separate development of pollution control legislation did not end when EPA was created. Congress continued to expand EPA's separate programmatic responsibilities. The most important expansion of EPA's statutory authority resulted from the passage of the 1972 Federal Water Pollution Control Act (FWPCA). Like the 1970 Clean Air Act, the passing of the FWPCA was influenced by the appearance of a critical Nader study, in this instance *Water Wasteland*, by

David Zwick and Marcy Benstock. Unlike the 1970 Clean Air Act, however, the FWPCA did not go unopposed by the White House. Sensing that its passage would not permit EPA to manage the environment comprehensively and anxious about the economic implications of additional water pollution regulations, the Nixon administration vetoed this bill. (For more details on the passage of this act, see Chapter 6.)[15]

The FWPCA changed the thrust of water pollution enforcement from state water quality standards to national discharge limitations. Under the act, the authority of the federal government was enhanced by a national system of emissions standards and permits. The theory behind it was that the general rules, contained in effluent guidelines, were supposed to be applied to particular plants when they were issued a permit by federal officials. The effluent guidelines would state the minimum standard that an entire industry category, such as grain mills, glass manufacturers, or petroleum producers, would have to achieve, while the permits would specify the limitation figure that a particular plant would have to accomplish. The intended result was that the permit writer would have national guidelines to support the numbers he demanded from industry and there would be little room for negotiation on a case-by-case basis. Similar cases would be treated alike, and there would be a uniform national policy to replace the divergent state laws, standards, and guidelines that had been in existence.

The conceptual basis for EPA's air and water pollution control programs was different.[16] The purpose of the water pollution program was to expand recreational possibilities. The purpose of the air pollution program was to protect the public's health and welfare. In air pollution, the major concern was controlling the long-term hazard to human health caused by various contaminants in the air, while in water pollution it was removing enough of the organic material from waterways to make them fishable and swimmable. Air pollution specialists were generally health scientists; water pollution specialists, generally engineers. The skills of one were not applicable to the problems faced by the other.

According to the Clean Air Act, national air quality goals were established based on health and welfare criteria; according to the water pollution act, national emissions limitations were established based on technological and economic feasibility. Even though they were in the same agency and for a time were in the same assistant administrator's office, the two programs were separate entities with different laws and operating procedures. Employees did not generally transfer from program to program because the programs confronted different issues and employees had different perspectives.

THE RESEARCH PERSPECTIVE

Those with program and policy perspectives had to engage in immediate practical activity. They had to issue regulations, make economic determinations, and achieve statutory deadlines by particular dates. They believed that in comparison to themselves research scientists enjoyed the luxury of an "ivory tower." There was a time perspective difference between bureaucrats with program and policy perspectives and bureaucrats who functioned as research scientists. Research scientists were discipline oriented. They saw their purpose as expanding the state of the art and making contributions to the environmental sciences that would have a long-term impact. Those with program and policy perspectives, however, had a need for immediately relevant information. They wanted detailed answers to specific questions and were not seeking ultimate answers to long-term problems.

The researchers were in touch with the work done by their professional counterparts in academia and industry. They maintained that since the environmental disciplines were undeveloped, pure research was more important than practical research. The needs of the programs and regions were too immediate and particular. They argued that these programs focused too much on technical support and service, on the knowledge and equipment that applied to unique problems.

Many of the in-house scientists were engaged in health and ecological effects research. It took time to measure actual discharges and emissions, to gauge human health effects in both the short (three to ten years) and long (twenty to forty years) term, and to trace ecological effects through the ecosystem for a number of generations.

Other researchers had gained competence in developing and demonstrating technology. They had a gradual, pragmatic approach. They chose the few worst offenders, where technological change would yield the greatest pollution control results and ignored all other industries. They worked on a program basis developing the basic theory of how to remove a chemical from the water and trying it out on a small scale. Only if the idea worked on a small-scale model, did they build a pilot plant. Only if the pilot plant could be perfected, did they initiate a larger project. Only if the larger project proved feasible, did they create a full-scale demonstration. Six months to a year could be spent on the pilot plant, two years on the larger project, and up to four years on the full-scale demonstration. Technological research required time, money, and patience.

Researchers, both technical and health and ecological, argued that from their perspective, the deadlines in the 1970 Clean Air Act and the 1972 Water Pollution Control Act were unrealistic. Dealing with changing national priorities was unproductive. From a scientific standpoint and from the perspective of scientific and technical disciplines, there was no extant definitive knowledge.

Spread out in laboratories throughout the United States, researchers mostly communicated with EPA programs through the mail, by distributing technical documents or by circulating briefings on issues and options. They had the freedom to do longer-term investigations while the other program bureaucrats dealt with immediate pressures.

The view of EPA bureaucrats was limited by the location they occupied in EPA's structure and by the tasks they had to perform. Those with a policy perspective made efforts to meet the challenge of shifting national priorities. The program managers sought to implement separate statutory provisions. Standard operating procedures prevailed at the program manager and operator level. The researchers had their own goals and timetables and their own tasks and priorities. Research scientists did specific projects that they believed would increase basic knowledge about natural and mechanical processes.

The Problem of Communication

In 1974, an EPA task force charged with defining an Office of Research and Development Planning Process and headed by Andrew Briedenbach, a director of one of EPA's labs, wrote:

Past experience with the Office of Research and Development has resulted in the rest of the agency viewing the Office of Research and Development as an independent self-serving operation rather than as an integral part of the agency.[17]

EPA's first assistant administrator for research, Stanley Greenfield, tried to deal with the problem of communication between researchers and the rest of the agency in a variety of ways. His responses to the problem can be divided into three categories: an organizational response, a system's response, and a division of labor response.

THE ORGANIZATIONAL RESPONSE

EPA inherited approximately fifty-six laboratories from old environmental programs.[18] The water research program was strongly oriented toward the development of technology for the treatment of waste from industrial and municipal sources. The air pollution research program was mostly concerned with health effects. In fiscal year 1972, the research office had a $165 million budget and 2,000 employees from sixty different scientific and professional disciplines and specialities who were dispersed in fifty-six labs located in eighteen states.

Greenfield's first effort was to create four National Environmental Research Centers (NERC) to consolidate data and coordinate research operations.[19] He tried to match NERC themes with the capability and major expertise of the existing laboratories. The Corvallis Oregon center, which included laboratories in seven locations throughout the United States, was supposed to be organized around *ecological effects*. The Cincinnati center, which had laboratories in three locations, was supposed to be organized around *pollution control technology*. The Research Triangle Park, North Carolina center, which had laboratories in four states, was supposed to stress *health effects*. Finally, Las Vegas, with laboratories in five locations, was supposed to emphasize research on *monitoring*.

The NERC themes did not develop as Greenfield hoped. They were a formal designation more than a reality. Before EPA's creation, Corvallis and Cincinnati had mostly water quality laboratories; Research Triangle Park, air pollution; and Las Vegas, a radiation center. To a large extent they retained their old identities rather than fitting into the new organizational scheme. Scientists, who had spent many years on specific projects, did not abandon them suddenly when headquarters called for a reorganization. The North Carolina center did not restrict itself to health effects, but continued to do work in all areas of air pollution. Cincinnati continued to stress water quality control. The Corvallis operation was not so much an ecology center as a collection of diverse laboratories that could not be fitted into any other category. Plans to consolidate and upgrade the labs were blocked by Congress which resisted the closing of outdated labs because they were community institutions that provided employment to local citizens.

THE SYSTEM'S RESPONSE

Greenfield's second response to the communications problem was to set up a needs planning system. Each year, the other assistant administrators and the regional administrators were supposed to submit a detailed list of their long-range and short-range needs to the research office. The research office would review the program needs and break them up into a number of projects which it would assign to the various laboratories. They then would produce reports, which would be sent to research headquarters in Washington. The Washington research office would then distribute these reports to the other offices and regions.

The researchers resisted the needs system. They feared that if properly implemented, it would give Washington too much control over their operations. They considered themselves independent professionals engaged in pure science as opposed to the scientists-at-headquarters who combined their calling with politics and management.[20] The field scientists argued for their autonomy. They maintained that scientists-at-headquarters should not control the day-to-day operations of labs in the field.

According to the laboratory researchers, EPA's first research priority should have been developing and upgrading the state of the art. The research scientists felt that if a new project were started every six months because of immediate needs and an overall long-term plan were not developed, the discipline of environmental sciences would never mature enough to cope with the difficult problems of the future.

Because they required very specific information, the program and regional offices that received the reports produced by the laboratories were often dissatisfied with the researcher's efforts. For example, a regional administrator in Colorado might want to know what were the ramifications from the runoff of alkaline soil into the area's rivers. His request for information would be combined with similar requests for information from other regions by the research office. Seeking to get as much knowledge for the fewest dollars possible, the research office would combine numerous program requests into a much smaller group of projects. The different questions about soil alkalinity and runoff would be perceived as a complicated problem that required three or four tasks in order for it to be solved. Some of these tasks might be assigned to in-house researchers and some might be contracted out. The total report would come back to the regional administrators who requested the information in pieces of varying quality. The pieces would examine the problem in general but would have little to say about the region's specific problem. Because of the irrelevant output they received, the regional and the program offices were dissatisfied with the "needs" system. They had numerous detailed "needs" that researchers were not satisfying.

THE DIVISION OF LABOR RESPONSE

Another means to solving the communications problem was to divide labor between research scientists and the program operators. The research scientists' role would be technology development and transfer. The program operators' function would be technology application. This method was used in regard to monitoring.[21] Researchers were supposed to solve the problem of standard analytical methods and design monitoring systems. Using flow charts they would figure out the part of the river, the portion of the air, and the industries on which equipment should be installed. They were supposed to provide program and regional offices with quality control procedures for surveillance required by statute. The program and regional offices were then supposed to apply these procedures by doing actual monitoring.

EPA depended on the institutional framework for surveillance that it inherited from existing state and local systems. Even after researchers developed new monitoring procedures, the state and local systems used different methods to collect data. In 1971, the agency did a study to see if it should centralize monitoring in one office thereby making it a support function; but programs, regions, and states complained about losing control over the monitoring function. They did not want to have to request this service, crucial to the performance of their task, from another office.

EPA retained the existing monitoring system, but the existing system data was slow in coming and analysis was time-consuming. The best data available at a given moment were almost always out of date. States and regions were deficient in applying the new monitoring methods. A 1973-74 study in the Midwest uncovered the following problems: (1) unacceptable analytic methods for some pollutants: (2) improper locations of monitoring sites and placement of instruments; (3) inadequate use and maintenance of instruments; and (4) unqualified operators and errors in data handling and calculation.[22]

The existing procedures generated statistics about violations that were useful to the enforcement function. It told how many states were in violation of air quality standards or how many industries were not complying with their permits. No one in the agency, however, had direct responsibility for moving from these figures about violations to figures about overall air and water quality. Instead of good estimations of air and water quality, the agency had relatively good estimations of regulatory compliance.

There were problems with definitions of air and water quality. Air quality was defined in terms of the emissions of six pollutants into the atmosphere: total suspended particulates, sulfur dioxide, carbon monoxide, photochemical oxidants, nitrogen dioxide, and hydrocarbons. Only these pollutants were regulated by national standards, but their discovery was made years ago, and there was no longer any certainty that they were still the most dangerous. In 1975, the Council on Environmental Quality admitted:

It is becoming increasingly evident that the air pollutants upon which our standards and monitoring have been focusing do not represent all important parameters of air quality. In some cases, they may not even represent the most important or informative ones.[23]

In water pollution there were sixteen general variables, fifteen trace metals, and twelve pesticides that were used for evaluation, but there were countless other factors that could have been taken into account. PCB's only had been discovered within the past ten years, and the list of water pollutants kept growing. Researchers did not develop satisfactory techniques and the states and regions did not gather accurate information pertinent to an estimation of overall environmental quality.

Summary

Some of EPA's bureaucrats were presidentially oriented and had a policy perspective; some were congressionally oriented and had a program perspective; and some were professionally oriented and had a research perspective. Those with a policy perspective defended the agency against charges that its actions were hurting the economy and contributing to energy dependence. Those with a program perspective carried out tasks and functions tied to specific statutes and appropriations. Those with a discipline perspective did long-term research that was more relevant to solving environmental problems of the future than it was to meeting the needs of bureaucrats with presidential and congressional perspectives.

Action was complicated because the bureaucracy was divided structurally into competing units, because bureaucrats perceived problems differently depending on their task and situation, and because bureaucrats who perceived problems differently did not communicate well with each other.

Notes

1. See unpublished papers by Ash Council Staff W.K. Tally (September 18, 1970) and W. Stitt (September 21, 1970) on functionalization.
2. Alain Enthoven, "A Functional Organization and Financial Plan for the Environmental Protection Administration," unpublished EPA document.
3. See Alain Enthoven and K. Wayne Smith, *How Much Is Enough: Shaping the Defense Program 1961-1969* (New York: Harper & Row, 1971).

4. For a description of Costle's role, see William R. Ahern, "Organizing for Pollution Control: The Beginnings of the Environmental Protection Administration, 1970-1971" (Cambridge, Mass.: John F. Kennedy School of Government, 1973).

5. Ibid, pp. 29-34.

6. See Richard Corrigan, "Agency Report/EPA Ending Year-Long Shakedown Cruise; Ruckelshaus Cast as Embattled Spokesman," *National Journal Reports* (October 9, 1971), pp. 2039-47.

7. He appointed Thomas Carrol—an Indiana friend with experience in radio, publishing, and broadcasting—assistant administrator for planning and management. He picked another close friend from Indiana, Donald Mosiman, a Republican lawyer who had managed his unsuccessful Senate campaign in 1968, to be assistant administrator of media programs. Ruckelshaus' third choice as assistant administrator was John Quarles, who had been a policy planner for Interior Secretary Hickel. Quarles headed the Office of General Counsel and Enforcement. Stanley Greenfield was appointed to direct the Research and Monitoring Office, and David Dominick, head of the old Federal Water Quality Administration, was promoted from the inherited bureaucracy to direct the categorical program office.

Ruckelshaus appointed a deputy administrator only after the basic organizational decisions had been made and other assistant administrators chosen. The deputy that he appointed, Robert Fri, had been brought to his attention by Fred Malek and the Domestic Council. Fri was a Harvard Business School graduate and management consultant who had been employed in the Washington office of McKinsey and Company. His management experience was supposed to compensate for Ruckelshaus' inexperience.

8. See Robert Gillette, "Environmental Protection Agency: Chaos or 'Creative Tension'?", *Science* (August 20, 1971), pp. 703-07.

9. See the theories and descriptions of bureaucratic behavior found in Herbert A. Simon, *Administrative Behavior*, 2nd ed. (New York: The Free Press, 1957); Peter M. Blau, *The Dynamics of Bureaucracy* (Chicago: The University of Chicago, 1963); Harold Seidman, *Politics, Position, and Power* (New York: Oxford University Press, 1970), pp. 37-64; Graham T. Allison, *Essence of Decision* (Boston: Little, Brown and Company, 1971), pp. 10-39, 67-101.

10. For complete information on EPA's legal authorities, see U.S. EPA, *Legal Compilation: Statutes and Legislative History, Executive Orders, Regulations, and Guidelines and Reports* (Washington, D.C.: U.S. Government Printing Office, 1973). A good summary of EPA's statutes (pre-1972) is provided by EPA, *The Challenge of the Environment: A Primer on EPA's Statutory Authority* (Washington, D.C.: U.S. Government Printing Office, 1972).

11. Rivers and Harbors Act of 1899, 33 U.S.C., Sections 403, 407, 411 (1899).

12. Air Pollution Act of July 14, 1955, P.L. 84-159, 69 Stat. 322.

13. Water Quality Act of 1965, October 2, 1965, P.L. 89-234, 79 Stat. 953; Motor Vehicle Air Pollution Control Act, October 20, 1965, P.L. 89-272, 79 Stat. 922; Air Quality Act of 1967, November 21, 1967, P.L. 90-148, 81 Stat. 485.

14. Clean Air Act, as amended, 42 U.S.C., Section 1857, et seq.

15. The Federal Water Pollution Control Act Amendments of 1972, 33 U.S.C., Section 1251, et seq. (Supp. 1975).

16. See "Water Quality Strategy Paper" (Washington, D.C.: EPA, 1975) and "Air Program Policy Statement" (Washington, D.C.: EPA, 1974). Also see Administrator's Special Task Force, Chairman Sam Hughes, "Report to the Administrator—Impact of Water Quality Legislation on the Environmental Protection Agency" (Washington, D.C.: EPA, April 1972).

17. Andrew W. Breidenbach, "Report of the Task Force to Define an Office of Research and Development Planning Process: Executive Summary" (Washington, D.C.: EPA, October 3, 1974).

18. See "Laboratory Plan for the Environmental Protection Agency" (Washington, D.C.: EPA, November 1972).

19. See Marian Jellinek, "Report on the Organization of Research and Development: Technical Information and Policymaking in the Environmental Protection Agency" (Washington, D.C.: Committee on Environmental Decision-Making, 1976).

20. See Walter Hirsch, *Scientists in American Society* (New York: Random House, 1968) and J. L. Pennock, Jr., et al., eds., *The Politics of American Science* (Chicago: Rand McNally, 1965).

21. On EPA's monitoring problems, see "Task Force Report: EPA Strategy for Managing Monitoring: Issues and Alternatives" (Washington, D.C.: EPA, February 18, 1972); "First Report of the Environmental Measures Project: Analysis and Applications of Environmental Quality Indicators" (Washington, D.C.: EPA, July 1975); "Surveillance and Analysis Division Study" (Washington, D.C : EPA, August 22, 1975); and "Air Pollution Indices Used in the United States and Canada" (Washington, D.C.: CEQ and EPA, December 1975).

22. See Council on Environmental Quality, *Environmental Quality: The Sixth Annual Report* (Washington, D.C.: U.S. Government Printing Office, 1975), pp. 336-37.

23. Ibid., p. 326.

5

Carrying Out Instructions: 1970 Clean Air Act

EPA's bureaucrats were divided into different divisions; they were separated by opposing professional allegiances; and they had to carry out different programs with diverse statutes, goals, and timetables. They were too divided to maximize intended consequences and minimize unintended consequences within a specified time period. Delay occurred in carrying out the instructions of Congress in both the 1970 Clean Air Act and the 1972 Federal Water Pollution Control Act. In both cases delay was a function of the complexity of joint action. Many participants and perspectives, many decision points, and the need to reach agreement among participants prevented the bureaucracy from achieving statutory goals in the timetables mandated by Congress.

The goal of the 1970 Clean Air Act was to achieve "healthy air" by 1975. Healthy air was defined as achieving primary health goals for six pollutants: particulate matter, sulfur dioxide, carbon monoxide, photochemical oxidants, nitrogen oxides, and hydrocarbons. The first two pollutants are mostly emitted from industrial smokestacks, while the latter are found primarily in motor vehicle exhaust. Photochemical oxidants or smog are formed by the combination of hydrocarbon and oxides of nitrogen in the presence of sunlight. The

Council on Environmental Quality alleges that these pollutants aggravate common respiratory and cardiovascular illness, can impair mental function, and can increase mortality.[1] One of them, hydrocarbons, is a suspected cause of cancer.[2]

Three months after EPA was created, the agency set national health standards for these six pollutants. By 1975, under the provisions of the 1970 Clean Air Act, it was supposed to achieve these standards. Although it met the initial deadline for setting the standards and it met subsequent deadlines for drafting state implementation plans to achieve air quality standards, it did not achieve healthy air in five years.[3] Five years after the Clean Air Act was passed, air quality had improved, but the Council on Environmental Quality conceded that healthy air had been fully attained in only 91 of the nation's 247 air quality regions. Air quality in major metropolitan areas, such as Baltimore, Boston, Detroit, Houston, Los Angeles, and Philadelphia, did not meet primary health standards. Only in relatively unpopulated rural areas, for example, Vermont and South Dakota, where air quality never had been below safe levels, were national health standards fully achieved.

Why wasn't the deadline for healthy air met? This was not an instance where Congress delegated vague standards to the bureaucracy, where it in essence said, "Here is a problem; deal with it." Unlike the antitrust division of the Justice Department and the Federal Trade Commission, which operate without a definite timetable, EPA had clear legal authority—a definite timetable, explicit goals, and unambiguous means to achieve its goals.

The participants in the effort to achieve healthy air included the general public, the White House, Congress, bureaucrats, the automobile manufacturers, EPA researchers, citizens, environmentalists, and local politicians. They had to make decisions about the costs of pollution control, its energy implications, auto company requests for extensions, and the use of transportation control plans. Making these decisions when numerous autonomous actors had to be accommodated led to delay.

The Costs of Pollution Control

One of the most important actors was the general public. How did the average American view the financial sacrifices that he was being asked to make for the sake of healthy air? The evidence indicates that most people were not willing to make significant sacrifices for this purpose.[4] Although polls in the early 1970s showed that a majority of the public believed that the government had not been spending enough for pollution control, these polls also indicated that most citizens were not willing to aid pollution control efforts by making significant sacrifices. Two-thirds of the public sampled in a 1969 poll done by the Opinion Research Center were not willing to spend $100 a year to control pollution. The Gallup organization in the same year found a majority in favor of increased pollution costs, only if the costs to the average citizen did not exceed $10 per year. Even in 1971, at the height of concern about the quality of the environment, as many as 40 percent of those polled indicated that they were not willing to spend anything for pollution control purposes.

EPA was born out of massive public agitation, moral fervor, and the backing of many political actors, and it tried to make a vigorous effort to achieve its goals in its early stages. However, the support built up during the period when its laws were gestating reached a climactic peak at the moment that its enabling legislation was passed. The agency assumed the burden of achieving statutory goals as interest in its mission began to wane. Statutory goals, no matter how explicit, paled in comparison with the enduring reluctance of the public to make significant sacrifices for the sake of healthy air. Support for EPA's goals of healthy air was neither long lasting nor deep. After 1971, only committed environmentalists supported without qualification all of the

1970 Clean Air Act's original provisions. James L. Sundquist concluded a discussion of another environmental issue, the "natural beauty" issue of the 1960s, by remarking

> ...it was evident as the decade ended that public interest could wane as well as wax...zeal mobilized was not...sustained...and the beautification advocates—who had only psychic income at stake—scarcely even tried to compete with those whose money income was in balance.[5]

The same waxing and waning of interest on the part of the public applied to pollution control.

Gradually, citizens became aware that the costs of pollution control were widely distributed. The American economy was locked into a pattern of rapid inflation and high unemployment that took its toll on every member of society. In 1973, an already serious economic situation was aggravated by the Arab oil embargo and resulting energy crisis. Prices soared and unemployment reached its highest level since the Great Depression. When it came to implementation of the 1970 Clean Air Act, citizens, affected by these events, began to perceive that they and not just industry and government would have to pay the costs for reducing pollution.

As the economy declined, bureaucrats became sensitive to citizens' reluctance to make sacrifices for the sake of pollution control. EPA officials recall that the events that occurred between 1972 and 1974 were of profound importance in regard to attaining the goal of healthy air. "Slowly, subtly, and without making a conscious decision," the agency began to alter its priorities in accord with economic and energy concerns.[6] This change in priorities was in line with the preferences of the White House, which was concerned about energy scarcity as well as the impact of pollution control on employment, growth, and inflation. It also was concerned about the costs to specific industries and dislocations in particular regions. The 1970 Clean Air Act had not required EPA to take any of these considerations into account. If EPA strictly adhered to the language in the 1970 statute, it would

disregard economic implications and judge emissions reduction requirements entirely on the basis of health and welfare
criteria. Fearing adverse economic impacts that might ac-
company pollution abatement, the White House wanted EPA
to balance costs against benefits.

To force EPA to consider economic factors, Office of Management and Budget (OMB) Director George P. Schultz
informed Ruckelshaus on May 21, 1971, that EPA regulations had to be cleared by OMB, other relevant agencies, and
the Commerce Department before being promulgated.[7] The
Commerce Department then tried to use this right of clearance to destroy the credibility of EPA regulations. It mobilized a group of economists, who challenged regulations if
insufficient economic analysis was done by EPA. When
Commerce Department challenges introduced evidence that
had not been considered, EPA had no choice but to modify
the regulations. In response to the gradual erosion of its
power, Ruckelshaus tried to improve the agency's capacity to
do economic analysis by organizing a steering committee
review process. Demonstrating to the White House that EPA
had a sound awareness of economic impact, however, was
not easily accomplished. When OMB or the Commerce
Department contested regulations on economic grounds,
Ruckelshaus often had to resort to legal argument. He tried
to make OMB and the other departments and agencies in the
government understand that some of the apparently extreme
measures that EPA was proposing were required by statute.
He argued that under the Clean Air Act, the administrator of
EPA and only the administrator was responsible for issuing
regulations. Commerce, OMB, and the White House did not
have the right to prevent EPA from proceeding for economic
reasons.

In contrast to the White House, Congress—a third significant actor—supported the idea that clean air was a fundamental value which could not be delayed because of the
economic impact of proposed EPA regulations. In hearings
held in 1972, members of Muskie's subcommittee argued that
the costs of pollution control were not relevant. Senator

Thomas Eagleton rebuked Ruckelshaus for permitting review of agency decision by OMB.

...at least some in your agency up until recently thought OMB called the final shots.... I hope that in the future that any influence on the Environmental Protection Agency insofar as promulgating regulations, guidelines, new source standards, and so forth, do come exclusively from within the agency and are not influenced by outside sources.[8]

Eagleton maintained that White House efforts to control the economic impact of regulatory decisions was not consistent with the intent of Congress.

In 1972, in testimony before the Senate Pollution Control Subcommittee, Richard Ayres, representative of the Natural Resources Defense Council, argued that OMB review would make it impossible to achieve air quality goals by 1975.

...it is becoming painfully clear that the promise of the clean air amendments will not be fulfilled. State implementation plans, which were to have been comprehensive blueprints for new action, have mostly become little more than weak-kneed apologies for each state's present program. Nearly two-thirds of the states we analyzed admitted openly that they could not reach at least one national standard. Most of the rest are so hobbled by other infirmities that their promises to meet standards cannot be taken seriously.[9]

He maintained that OMB review had emasculated state efforts.

The major blame for this situation must be placed squarely on the Nixon administration. The White House Office of Management and the Budget is reviewing in secret every major action of the Environmental Protection Agency. The public is completely excluded from this review, but the most anti-environmental Federal agencies, such as the Commerce Department and the Federal Power Commission, appear to have full access to it. These agencies, acting as spokesmen for industrial interests, have effective power to veto

EPA's actions. Now becoming routine, OMB review is gelding the Clean Air Amendments.[10]

Ayres alleged that before the review process, a non-deterioration provision favored by environmentalists was included among state implementation plan requirements. This provision prohibited the approval of plans that allowed "significant deterioration of existing air quality in any portion of any state." After OMB review, the non-deterioration provision was eliminated. Instead, states were urged "to consider the relative social and economic impacts of alternative control strategies."

After Nixon's 1972 election, Ruckelshaus stipulated that he would serve again as administrator only if the OMB review procedure was so clarified that final authority rested within EPA.[11] Nixon in a conversation with Ruckelshaus agreed, but his assurance did not affect the behavior of the White House staff, OMB, or the departments who continued to hold EPA accountable for economic impact.[12] Only in the summer of 1973 when Russell Train became EPA's second administrator did the agency obtain written confirmation from the White House that the administrator held ultimate authority over the content of the regulations it issued.[13]

Auto Pollution Extensions

Before the energy crisis of 1973, Muskie's pollution control subcommittee was opposed to granting the auto companies extensions of the five-year/90 percent auto pollution deadlines. When a 1972 National Academy of Sciences study, that took into account economic consequences, supported industry's claim that 90 percent reductions in five years could not be achieved, the Senate subcommittee sought to discredit the report.[14] Ruckelshaus on May 12, 1972, refused to grant the auto manufacturers an extension on the grounds that Congress did not intend that he consider cost. The manufacturers, however, appealed to the United States Court of Appeals for the District of Columbia.[15] On February 10, 1973, the court overturned Ruckelshaus' decision stating in a lengthy opinion that economic factors had to be given greater weight.[16] This decision broadened the basis of review in the case of auto emissions to competing cost factors and societal considerations. In April 1973, the administrator granted a one-year extension for hydrocarbons carbon monoxides, and carbon oxides.[17] Under authorization of the 1970 Clean Air Act, he promulgated less stringent interim standards for the two pollutants.

TABLE 11
Auto Exhaust Standards
(in grams per mile)

	1973 Standards	90% Reductions	Interim Standards	California Standards
Hydrocarbons	3.0	.41	1.5	.9
Carbon monoxide	28.0	3.40	15.0	9.0
Nitrogen oxides	3.1	.40	1.2	1.2

The standards required significant reductions of approximately 50 percent for the major auto pollutants, rather than the original 90 percent reductions called for by Congress. Subsequently, in July 1973, Robert Fri, who was acting administrator in the period between Ruckelshaus and Train, also granted the auto companies a one-year extension of the 1976 nitrogen oxides standard. In an effort to require motor vehicle manufacturers to install catalytic converters in some 1975 autos, Ruckelshaus and Fri promulgated more stringent interim standards for the state of California. These standards required reductions of close to 70 percent, but did not require that the agency achieve the original 90 percent reductions called for by Congress.

THE ENERGY CRISIS

In October 1973, the Organization of Petroleum Exporting Countries (OPEC) imposed an oil embargo on the United States.[18] A few months later it sharply increased the price of oil. In response to these events President Nixon proposed modifications to the 1970 Clean Air Act.[19] In his January 1974 energy message, he suggested that the interim 1976-77 auto emissions standards be extended until 1977-78 so that manufacturers could concentrate on improving fuel economy. He also asked that the air quality standards for sulfur dioxide be temporarily lowered so that power companies could switch to coal and decrease American reliance on foreign oil.

To meet the emissions standards then in effect, the automakers had taken a number of steps that reduced the fuel economy in 1973-74 autos by about 10 percent over that of 1970 autos.[20] For compacts the reductions were 6 percent, and for standard and luxury size autos the reductions were 15 percent. However, a large percentage of the losses in fuel economy of 1973 and 1974 autos was caused by the retarded spark timer used to control hydrocarbons and carbon monoxide emissions and the exhaust gas recirculation that controlled nitrogen oxides. EPA officials believed that if the auto companies used catalytic converters instead of these techniques, there would be virtually no fuel penalty.[21]

Heavier automobiles were the most important reason for increased fuel consumption. In addition, the fuel penalty for air conditioners was 9 to 20 percent and the penalty for automatic transmissions was approximately 7 percent. Why did the president choose to delay air pollution reductions? Why didn't he try to reduce the weight of cars or restrict the use of air conditioners and automatic transmissions? Davies and Davies maintain that

the power companies, the automobile industry, and the coal and oil companies saw the energy crisis as an opportunity to weaken the provisions of the Clean Air Act.[22]

As a result of the energy crisis, automakers were faced with lower sales of their large "gas-guzzling" vehicles. Lower sales raised the prospect of increased unemployment in the industry. The automakers blamed pollution control requirements for their difficulties. Their employees, dealers, and advertising agents put pressure on Congress and on the White House, and this pressure had an impact.[23] The 1974 Energy Supply and Environmental Coordination Act extended the five-year/90 percent deadline another year until 1977 for hydrocarbons and carbon monoxide and until 1978 for nitrogen oxides.[24] It also gave the auto manufacturers the right to ask for another one-year extension of the deadlines for these pollutants and allowed utilities that switched to coal exemptions from pollution control requirements.

"ACID EMISSIONS"

Shortly after the 1974 Energy Supply and Environmental Coordination Act was passed, the Ford Motor Company asked for a third one-year extension, because sulfuric acid emissions had been discovered in the discharges of the catalytic converters. Ford brought the problem of "acid emissions" to EPA's attention in February 1973. This issue, however, remained dormant until the fall of that year when John Moran, an EPA research scientist in North Carolina, held an unauthorized press conference that alerted the public to the "danger." Moran, a health effects researcher located at Research Triangle Park—EPA's scientific complex near Durham, North Carolina—made public a study he had done that showed that although catalysts reduced hydrocarbons and carbon monoxide, they also caused significant amounts of sulfuric acid to be emitted with probable adverse effects on public health.[25]

Moran's study pointed out that the catalytic converter, which was supposed to eliminate the health hazards caused by air pollution, actually caused a health problem. The catalyst tended to convert the small amount of sulfur emitted from the engine as SO_2 into SO_3. The SO_3 combined with water vapor in the exhaust stream to form sulfuric acid, H_2SO_4, and other acid sulfates. Emissions of these sulfates by autos was minute, but in regions of high traffic density Moran was concerned that the level of sulfur emissions could become hazardous to health.

Moran's statements were attacked by EPA staff in Ann Arbor and Washington who held their own unauthorized press conference.[26] They accused Moran of leaking the information about health risks because he wanted EPA headquarters to continue funding his emissions testing program. They claimed that only under special circumstances were the emissions of sulfuric acid significant; otherwise sulfuric acid emissions were too small to make a difference. Only at sufficiently high concentrations were adverse health effects associated with sulfuric acid, but these high concentrations were not likely to occur.

The unauthorized press conferences took place in a transition period after Ruckelshaus left the agency and before Russell Train, who had been designated to succeed Ruckelshaus, had taken charge. Train confronted questions about the conflict during his nomination hearings, and he agreed to launch a program to resolve the issue of the health effects of sulfuric acid emissions.[27]

After Train became administrator, Moran's lab in North Carolina was given the authority to determine the comparative health effects associated with sulfuric acid emissions in relation to the health effects associated with hydrocarbon and carbon monoxide emissions. On January 30, 1975, it released the results of a study which estimated that the health risks from sulfuric acid emissions would exceed the benefits from reduced hydrocarbon and carbon monoxide emissions after four model years.[28]

The media again ran stories on the "acid emissions" problem, and Train felt that he had no choice but to grant the auto manufacturers another extension.[29] Train also supported an amendment to the 1974 law that would postpone achievement of the 1977 standards for hydrocarbons and carbon monoxide to 1982 and give EPA and industry more time to resolve the "acid emissions" controversy.[30]

Predictably, environmentalists criticized Train's decision as a sell-out, but surprisingly GM was also disappointed.[31] Unlike Ford and Chrysler, it had spent hundreds of millions of dollars on catalyst research, built an expensive plant for the fabrication of catalysts, and signed long-term contracts for obtaining the precious metals used in the catalyst.

Several studies immediately criticized Moran's report.[32] An environmental consulting firm hired by EPA and the trade associations for the catalyst manufacturers found that Moran's study overestimated sulfuric acid exposure levels by between 200 and 500 percent. The California Air Resouces Board rejected EPA's analysis and decided to adhere to the stricter 90 percent reduction timetable. Train responded by having EPA reevaluate its earlier report. In the reevaluation, EPA estimated that exposure to sulfuric acid would be more than one-third less than originally calculated. However, the agency still argued that after twelve model years the dangers from sulfur emissions would exceed the benefits of reducing emissions from other pollutants.

Transportation Control

With the three delays of the auto exhaust deadlines, air quality standards could be achieved by 1975 only if traffic was substantially reduced in regions that were not in compliance.[33] The phrase "transportation control" in the 1970 Clean Air Act, however, lacked any concrete meaning. In 1972, EPA officials created a list of twenty-five possible transportation control measures that included bicycle paths, parking restrictions, auto-free zones, gas rationing, gas taxes, mass transit construction, bus lanes, car pooling, and inspection maintenance programs.[34] The purpose of transportation control, no matter how it was defined, was to reduce the use of automobiles in large urban areas. Due to the difficulty of compelling citizens to reduce their driving, Ruckelshaus wanted to give states additional time to draw up transportation control plans. Ruckelshaus' strategy was for the agency to be tough on the auto companies, insisting that they meet the five-year/90 percent reductions, and easy on the driving public. From the perspective of continued public support, Ruckelshaus believed that this was the best policy EPA could follow. On May 21, 1972, after denying the auto companies' request for an extension of the 90 percent reductions, he granted seventeen of the most urbanized states a two-year transportation control extension.[35]

Ruckelshaus, however, could not carry out this policy of denying auto pollution extensions and delaying transportation control's imposition. As noted earlier, the Court of Appeals required Ruckelshaus to reconsider the original auto pollution extension decision. The municipalities of Riverside and San Bernardino in California, concerned about their severe auto pollution problem, then sued EPA to take away the extra time granted the states to impose transportation control; and a court order directed the agency to propose immediately a transportation control plan to meet statutory requirements for the state of California.[36]

The transportation control plan for the state of California required gas rationing in the city of Los Angeles.[37] Gas rationing meant issuing gas coupons and limiting the amount of gas produced for or shipped to the state. These measures were the only way to achieve the necessary 82 percent reduction in gasoline use during the high smog period of May to November. The proposal virtually would have shut down the entire auto transportation system in the city of Los Angeles, radically altering the citizens normal living patterns.[38] It was loudly condemned by local officials. Los Angeles Mayor Sam Yorty called it "asinine," "silly," and "impossible."[39] Yorty said, "I don't think you are going to be able to stop people from driving automobiles into the city."[40] Senator John V. Tunney (D.—Calif.) proclaimed:

I refuse to believe that the people of this great state must choose between public health and private transportation. This proposal aims at an environmental objective at the cost of economic and social chaos.[41]

Neither the politicans nor the citizens of California reacted favorably to a plan that would drastically curtail the public's ability to drive.

The National Resources Defense Council next sued to overturn the transportation control plan extensions that Ruckelshaus had granted to the other seventeen urbanized states. On January 31, 1973, the court ruled in favor of the NRDC, stating that the administrator of EPA had not shown sufficient cause as to why he granted the two-year transportation control extension. The court ordered the states that had been granted the extension to submit detailed plans in a few months' time.

Many states refused to develop their own plans. In these states, the federal government hired consultants—transportation contractors—to come up with transportation control plans. The contractors, hired by EPA and working out of its Washington headquarters, were not sensitive to local opinions and were not able to anticipate the resistance that developed to the transportation control plans they drafted.

At the state and local level few politicians could afford to support gas rationing or increased gasoline taxes and expect to be reelected. Some of the other alternatives were also not economically feasible. State and local officials maintained that the construction of additional mass transit systems was too expensive for most cities to undertake. Moreover, they maintained that there was not enough open space to build new mass transit systems. In addition, they argued that the plans, made in Washington by national authorities, did not take into account differing local conditions.

Local business people, taxi drivers, construction unions, and citizens also opposed forced reduction in automobile traffic. Businessmen feared that the inner city would experience even greater decline because of traffic restrictions. The taxi drivers and highway construction union officials felt that their livelihoods were threatened, and many citizens proclaimed that they would not use new bus lanes or public transportation routes.

The plan for New York City was fully approved by EPA. It included higher bridge tolls for cars coming into the city and bans on taxi cruising, but the city did not put the plan into effect. EPA had the legal authority to request that a state establish a transportation control plan but whether EPA also could *require* the state to implement the plan was a constitutional issue. Suits claimed that EPA did not have the constitutional power to force the states to pass transportation control legislation, and EPA's authority was upheld in some suits and struck down in others.

In Pittsburgh, a plan that called for exclusive bus lanes, staggered work hours, bridge tolls, increased parking fees, and emergency procedures to limit the number of autos in the central business district was condemned by local officials. County Commissioner Thomas J. Foerster proclaimed, "I personally believe that such a plan is unnecessary, self-defeating, and would lead to the death, rather than the clean up, of Pittsburgh's central business district."[42] The city planning director also blasted the proposals because he feared they would lead to a disastrous decline in central city economic activity.

In Massachusetts, EPA's regional office established a transportation control plan for the Boston area. Employers were expected to reduce employee parking, but EPA's regional office found that it could not enforce this portion of the plan. There were too many unsettled questions about the parking reduction proposals, and the regional office did not have sufficient personnel to monitor employers for compliance.

In New Jersey, there was a problem of sustaining the financial burdens of the transportation control program once it was started. New Jersey's plan called for an inspection maintenance system. Each driver was supposed to pay $1.60 to have his car inspected to see if it was running properly and controlling emissions. While the inspection cost was relatively small, 12 percent of the cars did not pass the test and over 10 percent checked had to have repairs that cost over $100. New Jersey also lost $2.40 on each inspection because of a wage and pension fund that the state-employed mechanics demanded. When drivers began to complain, state politicians abandoned this program.

In most localities traffic reduction plans were viewed as draconian and counterproductive. They were difficult to implement and administer. Los Angeles with its geographic dispersal, freeways, and lack of public transportation was a special case because its transportation control plan involved gas rationing, but no matter where transportation control plans were introduced they involved measures, such as car pooling, bus lanes, and inspection maintenance systems, that encountered problems. Car pooling depended on compatibility and citizen willingness to coordinate driving habits. The success of bus lanes relied on the premise that cars left at home would not be used for other purposes. An inspection program, which had the potential to achieve the greatest impact, had prohibitive administrative and financial costs. About ten million new cars covered by pollution control requirements were manufactured annually. At least 100 million other cars on the road escaped any regulation. Many were not tuned properly or their converters were not functioning, and they were emitting more pollutants than they might have.

Imposing transportation control to achieve the objectives of the Clean Air Act required changes that touched citizens in their daily lives. The goals of public health—lessening the impact of common cardiovascular illnesses, such as emphysema and heart disease—were in conflict with the average driver's concerns to get to work, go shopping, visit friends, and use his automobile without restrictions.[43]

The 1970 Clean Air Act gave EPA the right to impose transportation controls and to "legitimately coerce" the public for the sake of healthy air. When it came to driving restrictions, however, the government was unable to "legitimately coerce" the public to achieve what the Clean Air Act regarded as being in the public interest.

Summary

EPA did not achieve the healthy air goal in the time required by statute because of many decisions, many participants, and an inability to obtain agreement from the participants. Delay occurred in carrying out the 1970 Clean Air Act because clearance could not be obtained from crucial actors whose cooperation was essential to the program's success. If the general public had been willing to make the financial sacrifices necessary for reducing pollution, if the White House had not insisted on balancing costs against benefits, if the auto manufacturers had not requested extensions, if the courts and an EPA researcher had not acted in behalf of the auto company requests, if local citizens and politicians had not opposed traffic control plans, then healthy air would have been achieved. The goal was not achieved because of opposition from these actors during various phases of the implementation process.

Notes

1. Council of Environmental Quality, *Environmental Quality: The Sixth Annual Report* (Washington, D.C.: U.S. Government Printing Office, 1975), pp. 221-22.

2. Ibid.

3. Ibid. pp. 229-304; see also James A. Noone, "Environmental Report/ Doubts About Clean Fuels Fail to Deter EPA, States on Air Pollution Battle Plans," *National Journal Reports* (June 24, 1972), pp. 1050-59.

4. See Walter A. Rosenbaum, *The Politics of Environmental Concern* (New York: Praeger, 1973), p. 15.

5. James L. Sundquist, *Politics and Policy* (Washington, D.C.: The Brookings Institution, 1968), p. 381.

6. John Quarles, *Cleaning Up America* (Boston: Houghton Mifflin, 1976), pp. 193-95.

7. George P. Schultz, *Memorandum on Agency Regulations* (OMB, October 5, 1971).

8. U.S. Senate, Committee on Public Works, Subcommittee on Air and Water Pollution, Hearings, *Implementation of the Clean Air Act Amendment of 1970—Part I* (Washington, D.C.: 1972), pp. 324-25.

9. Ibid., p. 4.

10. Ibid.

11. Quarles, *Cleaning Up America*, p. 117.

12. Ibid., p. 118.

13. Ibid., p. 119.

14. See Charles O. Jones, *Clean Air* (Pittsburgh: University of Pittsburgh Press, 1975), p. 255, and Committee on Motor Vehicle Emissions, *Semi-Annual Report* (Washington, D.C.: National Academy of Science, January 1, 1972), pp. 39, 49. Reprinted in Senate Hearings, Part 3, pp. 1153-1237.

15. See R. Kaspar, "Auto Emission Standards Suspension" (Washington, D.C.: Committee on Environmental Decision Making, 1976). Also see "Hearing on Motor Vehicle Pollution Control" (Washington, D.C.: EPA, May 6-7, 1971).

16. Quarles, *Cleaning Up America*, p. 189.

17. See Kaspar, "Auto Emission Standards" Also see Frank P. Grad, Albert Rosenthal, et al., *The Automobile and the Regulation of Its Impact on the Environment* (Norman, Okla.: University of Oklahoma Press, 1975), pp. 340-64.

18. See James A. Noone, "Environment Report/Energy Issues Threaten Recent Environmental Gains," *National Journal Reports* (March 2, 1974), pp. 305-08, for the effect of the energy crisis on clean air goals.

19. See "President Nixon's Statement and Message on Energy" found in Council on Environmental Quality, *Environmental Quality: The Fifth Annual Report* (Washington, D.C.: U.S. Government Printing Office, 1974), pp. 545-64. Also see Stan Benjamin, "EPA Would Ease Clean Air Goals," *Boston Globe* (March 23, 1974), p. 1, and "Nixon Men Compromise on Amending Clean Air Act," *New York Times* (March 23, 1974).

20. See "A Report on Automotive Fuel Efficiency" (Washington, D.C.: EPA, February 1974).

21. In a 1974 report NAS concluded that the original 90 percent reductions could be met by autos equipped with catalysts without sacrificing fuel economy, but further reductions would demand at least some sacrifice in fuel economy. By using the catalyst to meet the 1975 United States standards, the auto companies would be able to match the fuel economy of both their uncontrolled 1967 vehicles and their regulated 1970 vehicles. By switching to catalysts instead of employing techniques that reduced gasoline mileage, the auto companies would actually improve fuel efficiency at the same time they tightened the control of pollution. See Quarles, *Cleaning Up America*, p. 194, and Committee on Motor Vehicle Emissions, *Semi-Annual Report* (Washington, D.C.: National Academy of Sciences, Febraury 12, 1973).

22. J. Clarence Davies and Barbara Davies, *The Politics of Pollution*, 2nd ed. (Indiananpolis: Bobbs-Merrill, 1975), p. 56.

23. Quarles, *Cleaning Up America*, pp. 192-93.

24. Energy Supply and Environmental Coordination Act of 1974, P.L. No. 93-319, Section 3, 88 Stat. 248 (1974) (codified at 42 U.S.C., Section 1857 c-10 [Supp. v. 1975].

25. Quarles, *Cleaning Up America*, p. 191.

26. Ibid. Quarles relates that "personality conflicts became entangled with scientific uncertainties."

27. See Committee on Public Works, United States Senate, *Nomination of Russell E. Train Hearings* (August 1, 1973).

28. See Theodore Bogosian, "Automobile Emissions Control: The Sulfate Problem (A)" (Cambridge, Mass.: John F. Kennedy School of Government, 1975), p. 15.

29. See "Applications for Suspension of 1974 Motor Vehicle Exhaust Emission Standards: Decision of the Administrator" (Washington, D.C.: EPA, March 5, 1975).

30. See Train's letter to Jennings Randolph, chairman, Committee on Public Works, where he approves the Ford administration's proposal.

31. See Theodore Bogosian, "Automobile Emissions Control: The Sulfates Problem (Sequel)" (Cambridge, Mass.: John F. Kennedy School of Government, 1975), p. 3.

32. Ibid., pp. 3-9.

33. See Quarles, *Cleaning Up America*, p. 201. John Quarles comments that by 1973

environmentalism had lost much of its early glamour and henceforth would have a struggle for public support. Between the comprehensive statutes enacted and the shifting forces of public opinion, the Environmental Protection Agency was about to be caught in the crunch.

The "crunch" was transportation control.

34. See "Transportation Controls to Reduce Automobile Use and Improve Air Quality in Cities" (Washington, D.C.: EPA, November 1974); "Cleaning the Air While Keeping the Car," *National Journal Reports* (January 3, 1976), pp. 8-12; and "Bicycle Transportation" (Washington, D.C.: EPA, December 1974).

35. *Federal Register*, 37, no. 105 (May 31, 1972), p. 10844. See Jones, p. 269.

36. Quarles, *Cleaning Up America*, p. 201.

37. See Jones, *Clean Air*, p. 270.

38. Quarles, *Cleaning Up America*, p. 202.

39. Jones, *Clean Air*, p. 270.

40. Ibid.

41. Ibid.

42. Ibid.

43. Quarles, *Cleaning Up America*, p. 203.

6

Carrying Out Instructions: The 1972 Federal Water Pollution Control Act

When Congress passed the 1972 Federal Water Pollution Control Act, it gave EPA instructions to achieve six deadlines: (1) by 1973, it was supposed to issue effluent guidelines for major industrial categories; (2) by 1974, it was supposed to grant permits to all water pollution sources; (3) by 1977, these sources were supposed to install the best practicable water pollution control technology; (4) by 1981, the major waterways in the nation were supposed to be fishable and swimmable; (5) by 1983, polluting sources were supposed to install the best available technology; and (6) by 1985, all discharges into the nation's waterways were supposed to be eliminated.[1]

The 1973 effluent guideline deadline was the cornerstone of an ambitious program to eliminate all pollution from the nation's waterways. EPA had to produce guidelines by October 1973 that were supposed to indicate the "best practicable technology" (BPT) for an industry in 1977 and the "best available technology (BAT) for an industry in 1983.[2] It was crucial that the guidelines appear in 1973, because they were supposed to be the basis for permits that had to be issued to all industrial pollutors by December 1974. The theory behind the 1972 Water Pollution Control Act was that the general rules, contained in the effluent guidelines, were to be applied to the particular permit cases. The effluent guidelines would state the BPT and BAT standard that an entire industry category, such as grain mills, glass manufacturers, or petroleum producers had to achieve, while the permits would specify the pollution allowable for a particular plant.

Although the proposal to pass a new water pollution control act was introduced in Congress in 1970, it was not passed till 1972. Before the act was passed, EPA carried out interim strategies. These strategies lost momentum and were postponed. Once the act was passed, the effluent guidelines did not appear on time. As of October 1973, not one effluent guideline had been promulgated.

The rational model of policy implementation assumes that bureaucracies adhere closely to the instructions they receive and that they are able to maximize intended outcomes within a specified time period. The reality is that bureaucracies stray from the instructions they receive because of the existence of numerous independent actors, many decisions, and the need to obtain agreement from these participants before proceeding.

The Passage of the 1972 Federal Water Pollution Control Act

President Nixon in his February 10, 1970, message on the environment recommended that Congress pass a new water pollution bill with provisions that included effluent guidelines.[3] The Senate Pollution Control Subcommittee under Senator Muskie held hearings on this proposal in the spring of 1970, but it took no action until a year later when it held general oversight hearings and reported out a bill.[4] This bill proclaimed that the discharge of pollutants into navigable waters had to be eliminated by 1985 and that

wherever attainable, an interim goal of water quality which provides for the protection and propagation of fish, shellfish, and wildlife and provides for recreation in and on the water should be achieved by 1981.[5]

These sweeping policy goals, and the bill's disregard for the economic implications of its proposed actions alarmed the White House. The White House appealed to the House Public Works Committee to reopen hearings on the bill, but the committee did not hold hearings till December 1971— almost eight months later. The bill that the committee finally reported to the full House modified the original one. It made the 1981 and 1985 goals dependent on further congressional action. The House passed this bill on March 29, 1972.

The Conference Committee then had to meet to resolve the separate House and Senate versions of the bill. It did so from May 11 to September 14, 1972. In all it met forty times trying to decide the issues of whether the 1981 fishable and swimmable goal and the 1985 zero-discharge goals were mere guidance as the House intended or actual policy as the Senate intended. The final Conference Committee compromise declared the 1981 and 1985 deadlines as "national goals" as provided by the House, not "policy" as voted by the Senate.[6] This difference, a mere sematic one, reflects the confusion and inability of Congress to make a final determination on the issue.

The Conference Committee's compromise bill was approved by both the House and the Senate on October 4, 1972, but, on October 17, 1972, John Erlichman delivered the president's veto. The White House was opposed to the sweeping goals of the bill, the timetables, and the bill's disregard for economic cost. The president, though, did not have the votes to sustain his veto, and the House and Senate voted by overwhelming majorities to override it.

Interim Strategies

Before the passage of the 1972 Federal Water Pollution Act, EPA had a two-pronged strategy for reducing water pollution which consisted of suing pollution control violators and issuing permits to firms to get them to achieve state water quality objectives.

THE SUIT STRATEGY

Between 1970 and 1972 EPA referred 371 enforcement actions to the Justice Department.[7] The agency brought criminal actions against Allied Chemical, Gulf Oil, Cities Service, Jones and Laughlin Steel, Minnesota Mining and Manufacturing, Mobil Oil, Republic Steel, Texaco, and United States Steel. It brought 169 criminal actions, 106 civil actions, and 96 actions for failure to apply for a permit.

The suit strategy encountered problems. One problem was the size of the Enforcement Office. Although the agency's zealous stand (see Chapter 3) aroused the interest of numerous young lawyers, who identified with EPA's environmental mission and were attracted by Ruckelshaus' judicial activism, the Enforcement Office still had trouble gathering a staff. Its total personnel and budget, in fact, made it the smallest office in the EPA. Its small size was attributable partially to the lack of employees that it inherited from the old programs, which had few enforcement positions.

The new attorneys attracted to the Enforcement Office by Ruckelshaus' suit campaign prepared close to 400 cases between 1970 and 1972, but like other agency and department attorneys these lawyers could not bring their cases to court. They only had the right to refer cases to the Justice Department for prosecution. The Justice Department attorneys who actually argued EPA cases were held back by the low level they occupied in the Justice hierarchy, and EPA attorneys could not always have cases argued for the sake of the principles they wanted to establish.[8]

To the extent that the Enforcement Office did inherit personnel from the old programs, they were located primarily in EPA's regional offices. Enforcement was supposed to be more decentralized than other offices of the agency because the action was at the local level where the offending industries could be found and brought to justice. The agency could not bring one large suit against all the violations of a large steel producing or chemical company that had plants in many locations. It had to bring individual suits against each particular plant.

The enforcement process was further limited because localities were fearful of losing industry. State agencies conducted the initial investigations to determine if the plant was in violation, but their resources were limited and generally they could not afford to have a company leave their state because of an aggressive enforcement posture. When there were obvious violations, EPA tried to get state agencies to take the necessary action. If after three months, the state did not inaugurate an appropriate enforcement action, the regional office of EPA took the case. It too had local connections and to some extent had to cooperate with local officials and industries.

If EPA's regional administrator wanted to take action, he had to receive prior approval from headquarters. It was obviously crucial that different regional offices not treat the same industry differently. If a lumber company, for example, was sued in Oregon for the same activities that it was permitted in Maine, then the suit had little chance of success and great chance of embarrassment for the agency. EPA's headquarters, which tried to maintain a consistent posture throughout the country, was also held back from pursuing violators by possible variations in local practices.

Another problem that the agency encountered was that the adverse publicity from the suits did not induce immediate compliance. Many companies for various reasons did not care about the bad publicity, especially if they did not directly sell to consumers. In addition, the media did not cover most of the suits after the first group was initiated. Only the *Wall Street Journal* continued to report on the progress of court cases. Once a pollution suit was brought and publicity receded, corporate lawyers delayed the proceedings because expenditures for pollution control were postponed as long as the case dragged on in the courts.[9]

Enforcement cases took a long time to complete and changes in company behavior rarely were forthcoming. Court actions were lengthy because of long court dockets, complex pre-trial procedures, the opportunities that the opposing counsel had for delay, the time and effort attorneys had to spend preparing cases for trial, and other difficulties that arose in pushing a case through to adjudication.[10] The judicial process was long and cumbersome, and outcomes were not predictable.

Further delay was created by appeal.[11] In many instances, formal administrative and court proceedings dragged on for years, during which time there was no pollution abatement. To cut short this lengthy and unproductive judicial activity, EPA and the Justice Department often resorted to negotiated settlements in which offenders would agree to partial clean-up programs, but adherence to these settlements often became the subject of further disputes with abatement deferred even longer.

The hopes raised by bringing suits against pollutors were not fulfilled. The negotiations and pre-trial work did not produce results before October 1972, the date Congress enacted new water pollution legislation. After October 1972, cases were held in abeyance.

The vastness of the water pollution problem, its dispersal in localities reluctant to have the law enforced, EPA's small staff, and the lack of publicity limited the effectiveness of a strategy that depended on civil and criminal suits against violators to obtain compliance. The actions necessary to achieve compliance were too complex, involving as they did diverse and autonomous actors—EPA bureaucrats, Justice Department officials, state agencies, regional EPA offices, media, company attorneys, and courts—each with the potential to block program progress.

PERMITS

The other strategy the EPA used to control water pollution in the 1970-72 period before passage of the Federal Water

Pollution Control Act was the issuing of permits. Permits were legal contracts that placed a company in an appropriate category, included a detailed time schedule for the installation of new equipment or for a change in industrial process, described a surveillance procedure, and portrayed the legal actions that could be taken against the company if it violated state water quality requirements. The federal government based the permit program on an 1899 Refuse Act that required all sources that discharged into a waterway to apply for a permit.[12] Representative Henry Reuss, the Council on Environmental Quality, and conservation groups urged the president to use this measure for pollution control purposes. Under the provisions of the Refuse Act, all discharges into navigable waters or their tributaries were subject to the conditions of such a permit.

On December 23, 1970, Russell Train, then chairman of the Council on Environmental Quality, announced the establishment by the president of a permit program based on the 1899 Refuse Act. Although the Commerce Department favored this approach, the program was not supported by the other interested actors. According to John Quarles, Congress was "chagrined" that the program was initiated without its approval; state agencies "livid" because the permits might supersede requirements set under the 1965 Water Quality Act; and many industries "aghast" at the sudden imposition by the president of a system involving demands for information about their discharges.[13] Environmentalists also were displeased. They feared that industries could not be trusted to submit honest discharge reports and that the permits issued might be too lax.[14]

Establishing the permit program was controversial with many of the groups the program depended upon for its success. The Refuse Act was also under jurisdiction of the Army Corps of Engineers. In addition to the program's being controversial, EPA had to share its administration with another government agency. EPA set up a Refuse Act Permit Program Office, and it hired contractors to identify various industries and the wastes they discharged, but the use of contractors further slowed progress. Still EPA was able to initiate industrial waste studies and to establish a format for the permit program that included application and review procedures. However, on July 1, 1971, when the first 50,000 applications from water polluting industries were due, only 3,000 had arrived. Most companies simply did not submit their applications on time.

Newsweek and the *Wall Street Journal* suggested that the program was collapsing.[15] Obviously without company cooperation, it had no chance of succeeding. To get companies to comply, the Enforcement Office announced lawsuits against the companies that failed to comply. By November 1971, another 12,000 applications were received and most of the 2000 or 3000 large dischargers had applied for a permit. Even so, EPA's review of the individual application forms revealed "glaring inadequacies" in the information the companies submitted.[16] In some forms, many questions were not answered, and in many instances the forms did not contain the information EPA needed to set limitation figures.

The permit program encountered many difficulties, but in July 1971 after 23,000 applications had been filed and a few permits issued, the program suffered a final blow. It was brought to a halt by a district court decision in Ohio that ruled the permit program was subject to the requirements of the National Environmental Policy Act. EPA was "overwhelmed" by the prospect of having to draft environmental impact statements for the 50,000 permits it had to issue.[17] It did not have the personnel to carry out such a task and appealed the court order, but in the meantime the issuance of permits was forbidden. For nearly a year, the permit program was held in abeyance because of this court order, which used the provisions of a National Environment Policy Act against the Environmental Protection Agency.

Before the 1972 Federal Water Pollution Control Act was passed, both methods that EPA used to control water pollution—suits and permits—had been delayed because of court action and the judicial process. The momentum behind the suit strategy diminished as more suits became lodged in lengthy judicial proceedings, and the permit program stopped operating because of an adverse court decision.

Effluent Guidelines

The passage of the 1972 Federal Water Pollution Control was supposed to give new life to the water pollution program. The Ohio court order prohibited EPA from using the Refuse Act to run a permit program, but the authority to run such a program as well as the authority to issue effluent guidelines were incorporated into the 1972 Federal Water Pollution Control Act. Under the 1972 Water Pollution Control Act, EPA had the authority to control pollution from over 200,000 industrial sources. To regulate 200,000 industrial pollutors required information about the discharges, manufacturing processes, and technical options of diverse firms operating in different circumstances throughout the country. Water pollutors were divided by EPA into more than 30 categories and 250 subcategories on the basis of product, age, size, and manufacturing process. They manufactured everything from asbestos and beet sugar to steam electricity and textiles. The bureaucracy found the task of regulating 200,000 diverse pollutors difficult to complete in the time allotted by Congress.

The 1972 Federal Water Pollution Control Act's eighty-nine single-spaced pages "presented a bewildering array of requirements."[18] It took several months for EPA officials to read the statute, debate its ambiguities, and set a strategy for carrying out the program. The most immediate deadlines— October 1973 when effluent guidelines had to be promulgated and December 1974 when permits had to be issued—gave bureaucrats additional work that they found difficult to handle.

The existence of these deadlines frustrated White House efforts to have the environment managed comprehensively and at the least cost. Burdened with these specific deadlines, the agency's employees did not have the time to view the environment in light of competing priorities. They did not have the time to conduct economic analysis because the

provisions of the 1972 FWPCA had to be carried out immediately. Effluent guidelines drafted and promulgated by the
bureaucrats inherited from the old programs were not subject to the same kind of review the steering committee had
been giving air pollution regulations.

Too many guidelines had to be issued in too short a time for
the steering committee to maintain intensive review. Authority was delegated to working groups directed by program
managers. The guidelines, not influenced by the direct involvement of the administrator, also were not sharpened by
conflict between EPA offices. Options were not generated
and the administrator did not achieve the same control over
decision-making as he had achieved in the case of air pollution regulations.

The program managers who carried out the 1972 Federal
Water Pollution Control Act encountered four problems in
their effort to meet congressional deadlines: (1) lack of
research participation; (2) shortage of time to generate and
evaluate information; (3) inconsistency between guidelines
and permits; and (4) appeals.

RESEARCH'S LACK OF PARTICIPATION

In May 1972, EPA's water program office created an Effluent Guidelines Division to gather the information needed to
implement what was at the time only proposed water pollution legislation. The only regulations similar to effluent
guidelines that the EPA previously had produced were a
handful of new source performance standards it had issued
under authority granted it by the 1970 Clean Air Act. It
lacked experience in directly regulating industry's emissions
or effluents. In order to produce the new water pollution
regulations, the Effluent Guidelines Division needed to bor-
row personnel from other offices. It wanted to reclaim technical and scientific personnel it had lost to the Office of
Research when the agency partially eliminated the old programmatic offices.

One of the reasons why EPA was supposed to be superior to other regulatory agencies was that it had an in-house research capability. EPA could rely on its in-house scientists to get data instead of relying on industry for information. If the Office of Research, however, did not participate in regulatory decision-making, then there was no advantage in having a research function housed in a regulatory agency. If it did not provide information that the Effluent Guidelines Division considered essential, it did not contribute to a common regulatory endeavor.

While the effluent guideline regulators had to apply existing knowledge, the scientists and engineers in the Office of Research were trying to expand the frontiers of existing knowledge (see Chapter 4). The regulators felt that the researchers were not supporting their regulatory endeavor, while the researchers defended the limits of their knowledge. They argued that the agency had given them regulatory tasks that they could not perform. From their perspective, the deadlines in the 1972 Water Pollution Control Act were unrealistic.

LACK OF TIME TO GATHER AND EVALUATE INFORMATION

Because of the time required to collect and evaluate information none of the effluent guidelines appeared on time. Most of what the Effluent Guidelines Division knew was general in nature and based on outdated or secondhand descriptions. It needed additional information provided by scientific and engineering professional associations. Members of the division visited plants throughout the country. The information they gathered was tabulated and put into a computer program. It showed that for most industrial categories no single plant had developed best practicable or best available technology. Each plant might have a special feature that functioned well. In order to ascertain what an industry could achieve, the agency had to bring together the diverse procedures of plants operating under different circumstances throughout the country.

The division hired contractors to help gather the data and make these judgments.[19] The contractors, who relied on observations of current industrial practice, had to establish the state of the art in various industries. They did business with industries EPA regulated and had to be carefully monitored by EPA lest they provide misleading information. The agency had to check if the contractors sampled the right proportion of plants, if they handled data properly, and if they looked carefully at all the factors involved.

Many companies—knowing what the data would be used for—were reluctant to give it to the contractors. When they resisted, the information had to be discovered in public records, or a company had to be served an administrative order requiring it to produce the information. In either case, there was delay. The contractors were given nine months to develop reports, but some took as long as two or three years to complete them.

Without completed reports the Effluent Guidelines Division was reluctant to make recommendations. Even when it received reports on time, the information did not provide conclusive answers to questions about the reliability of treatment technologies. There were too many distinctions in plants based on geography, size, and raw materials to arrive at a single best practicable or best available technology figure. Given the uncertainties involved in calculating these figures, the division had reason for delay. It had to be pressured into releasing guideline figures by the National Resources Defense Council. The environmental group sued EPA for delay and by January 1974, 38 guidelines for over 30 categories and 100 subcategories were promulgated.

INCONSISTENCY BETWEEN GUIDELINES AND PERMITS

The 1972 Federal Water Pollution Control Act hoped that the general rules, contained in the effluent guidelines, could be applied to particular permit cases. This was not possible. The particular case (the permit) and the general rule (the guideline) were developed simultaneously by different assis-

TABLE 12
Status of Effluent Guidelines, June 1975*

Industry groups	No. of sub cate- gor- ies	Court ordered date for promulga- tion	Date proposed	Date promul- gated	Law Suit
Group I, Phase I					
Fiberglass	1		8-22-73	1-22-74	1
Beet sugar	1		8-22-73	1-31-74	1
Feedlots	2		7-7-73	2-14-74	1
Glass	6		9-7-73	2-20-74	1
Cement	3		9-7-73	2-20-74	1
Phosphates	3		10-17-73	2-21-74	3
Rubber	4		10-11-73	2-22-74	5
Ferroalloys	3		10-18-73	2-26-74	1
Asbestos	7		10-5-73	2-28-74	1
Meat	4		10-30-73	3-12-74	3
Inorganics	22		10-11-73	3-20-74	22
Cane sugar	2		10-29-73	3-20-74	4
Grain mills	6		10-11-73	3-21-74	3
Fruits and vegetables	5		11-30-73	3-28-74	3
Electro- plating	1		12-7-73	4-5-74	3
Plastics and synthetics	13		11-9-73	4-8-74	12
Nonferrous	3		12-4-73	4-9-74	2
Fertilizers	5		12-26-73	4-12-74	20
Leather tanning	6		4-8-73	4-18-74	2
Soap and detergent	19		12-14-73	4-25-75	—
Timber products	8		12-20-73	5-9-74	2

*Council on Environmental Quality, *Environmental Quality 1975* (Washington, D.C., U.S. Government Printing Office, 1975), pp. 63-64.

TABLE 12
Continued

Industry groups	No. of sub-categories	Court ordered date for promulgation	Date proposed	Date promulgated	Law Suit
Organic chemicals	3		12-7-73	5-9-74	12
Petroleum refining	5		1-15-74	5-28-74	5
Builders paper	1		12-17-73	5-29-74	—
Dairy	11		1-14-74	6-26-74	—
Pulp and paper	5		2-6-74	6-28-74	12
Seafood	14		1-3-74	7-5-74	—
Iron and steel	12		2-19-74	10-8-74	5
Textiles	7		2-5-74		2
Steam electric	4		3-4-74		28

Group I, Phase II

Glass	6	11-15-74	8-21-74	1-16-75	
Rubber	7	11-12-74	8-23-74	1-10-75	
Meat	6	12-4-74	8-28-74	1-3-74	
Timber	7	11-12-74	8-26-74	1-16-75	
Asbestos	4	11-22-74	8-29-74	1-9-75	
Grain mills	4	12-5-74	9-17-74	1-3-75	
Plastics and synthetics	11	12-2-74	9-20-74	1-23-75	
Fertilizer	2	12-30-74	10-7-74	1-14-75	
Phosphates	3	1-8-75	1-27-75		
Ferroalloys	5	1-20-75	2-24-75[1]		
Poultry	5	—	4-24-75		
Inorganics	41	1-31-75	5-22-75		
Seafoods	19	1-15-75	1-30-75		

154

TABLE 12
Continued

Industry groups	No. of sub-cate-gor-ies	Court ordered date for promulga-tion	Date proposed	Date promul-gated	Law Suit
Cane sugar	5	1-31-75	2-27-75		
Nonferrous	5	1-31-75	2-27-75		
Electroplating	3	1-31-75	4-24-75		
Organics	4	7-1-75			
Fruits and vegetables	51	10-15-75			
Pulp and paper	10	9-15-75			
Iron and steel Foundries Carbon and alloy	23	7-1-75			
Group II					
Furniture	4	3-24-75	4-14-75	6-2-75	
Asphalt paving	4	4-12-75	1-10-75		
Paint and ink	4	5-12-75	2-26-75		
Auto and other laundries	6	—			
Fish hatcheries	3	—			
Transporta-tion	7	—			
Converted paper	—	—			
Petroleum and gas extraction	4	9-1-75			
Steam supply	2	10-6-75			
Coal mining	4	—			
Water supply	15	—			

TABLE 12
Continued

Industry groups	No. of sub-categories	Court ordered date for promulgation	Date proposed	Date promulgated	Law Suit
Mineral mining	25	10-5-75			
Miscellaneous chemicals	8	12-1-75			
Ore mining and dressing	11	11-15-75			
Foods and beverages	66	—			
Clay and gypsum	11	—			
Machinery and mechanical products	15	12-15-75			
Concrete products	3	—			

tant administrators' offices relying upon separate information bases. The permits, which were supposed to rely on the guidelines for their numbers, were issued simultaneously with the guidelines.[20] By the December 1974 permit deadline, more than half of the estimated 47,000 required permits had been issued. Ninety-four percent of "major" dischargers had been issued permits before the guidelines even appeared.

Unlike the Effluent Guidelines Division that had to start from scratch, the Enforcement Office that issued the permits updated an existing information base. It used the old industrial waste studies done before the Federal Water Pollution Control Act was passed, the Refuse Act applications, and the abatement commitment letters it collected as the foundation for its new program. Enforcement did studies of existing waste water treatment technology using old research and any other documentation it could find. It worked with industry through trade associations and tried to verify the information industry supplied. In this way it produced its own version of the guidelines—interim guidance figures—that covered assorted industrial categories and were used as a basis for the permits it issued.[21]

By May 1973, when the Effluent Guidelines Division was supposed to produce official guidelines, the Enforcement Office had produced temporary guidance for twenty-two industrial categories. Like the final guidelines, these interim guidance figures used standard industrial classifications, described industrial processes, and set waste limitations. When it became clear that the official guidelines would not appear on time, Robert Fri, who was at that time acting administrator of EPA, gave the Enforcement Office the right to issue permits on the basis of these interim guidance figures.

APPEALS

The interim guidance figures, although never published in the Federal Register, were circulated throughout the agency including the regional offices. Industries were made aware of the interim guidance figures, which in many instances were more stringent than the actual guidelines that were finally promulgated. The conflict between guidance and guideline figures confused regulated companies unsure about how much pollution reduction they were actually expected to achieve. They contested the permits in over 2,000 adjudicatory proceedings.[22] One of the issues repeatedly raised in these proceedings was guideline/permit contradiction. Were limitations in permits derived from the more stringent interim guidance figures binding? The bureaucratic separation between the Enforcement Office and the Effluent Guidelines Division created a gap between the permit and the actual guideline figures that industry used to its advantage to delay compliance.

In addition to challenges launched against permits, more than 150 lawsuits were brought against the guidelines. Du Pont prepared its case while the agency was still developing its figures. It sued the day the effluent guidelines for the chemical industry were promulgated. Industries like Du Pont hired prestigious law firms and used engineering companies and trade associations to gather evidence and make their case. They challenged the guidelines even after making comments that led to substantial revisions.

The case of the corn millers against EPA is instructive.[23] EPA had changed the original numbers in response to industry comments, and it felt that it was being lenient and flexible when the original regulation was issued. The agency therefore was surprised when a petition of challenge was filed in the Eighth Circuit Court of Appeals. Legal briefs were submitted by two groups of corn millers—the "dry millers" and the "wet millers." (Wet millers used more water to grind corn into flour and contributed more pollution than the dry millers who used less water.) The legal brief submitted on behalf of the dry millers by the Corn Refiners' Association and a few of the producers illustrated the standard issues. It claimed that EPA did not have the statutory jurisdiction to set specific numerical requirements; "guidelines" meant a range of figures and not single numbers. In addition, the permit writer, not the issuer of effluent guidelines, was the only one who had the legal right to set a limitation for a particular plant. The legal brief submitted by the wet millers argued that EPA ignored important cost factors; that it did not consider the enormous variability in waste load from day-to-day and from week-to-week; and that it should have included more subcategories to account for different processes and circumstances.

The industry lawyers made their arguments in extraordinarily long, technical briefs. The judge accepted the idea of EPA using single numbers but said that he did not have jurisdiction over the case and assigned it to a district court in

Des Moines, Iowa. The district court reviewed the new source standard for grain millers that was to go into effect in 1983 and said that the record was insufficient. The agency admitted that it had concentrated its attention on the 1977 part of the standard and had not focused as much attention on the 1983 requirement. It then revised this part of the regulation, but in new hearings industry continued to challenge the original 1977 goal. The district judge decided that EPA had to start again and rewrite the entire guideline. The agency appealed. It argued that the higher court had jurisdiction and that the district court's opinion was too vague to be used as a basis for rewriting the guideline. The process of appeal and counter-appeal meant that the guideline did not take effect and that the corn millers were able to delay indefinitely the installation of new technology.

Even standards developed with industry participation, such as the corn millers' guidelines, were delayed in the courts. Any effluent guideline could be challenged by industry lawyers on the basis of EPA's interpretation of the law. The lawyers could assert that EPA did not have the statutory authority to prescribe a single number, but that "guidelines" meant the agency had to establish a range of figures. Whether the regulation was sustained depended less on the capability of EPA regulators and the time and resources spent doing analysis and more on the arbitrariness of the particular court and the presiding judge involved.

Summary

Delays occurred in starting and carrying out the nation's ambitious program to reduce and ultimately eliminate pollution in the nation's waterways. The water pollution control bill introduced into Congress in 1970 was not passed immediately. Three decision points have been considered in discussing the delays encountered in implementing the 1972 Federal Water Pollution Control Act—one relating to the passage of the act itself; one relating to suit and permit strategies used before the act was passed; and one relating to the issuance of effluent guidelines and the granting of permits after the act was passed. In the instance of the passage of the act, delay was a function of White House intervention, House hearings, and Conference Committee sessions. In the instance of the suit strategy, delay was a function of a small, inadequate staff and the need to rely on Justice Department attorneys, state agencies, regional offices, the media, and company attorneys to insure compliance. In issuing permits, delay occurred because Congress, state agencies, industries, environmentalists, the Army Corps of Engineers, contractors, regulated companies, and the courts had to contribute and cooperate. After the act was passed, delay occurred in issuing effluent guidelines and in implementing the permit program based on the effluent guidelines because of the Research Office's lack of participation, a shortage of time to generate and evaluate the information provided by contractors, inconsistency between guidelines and permits, and numerous appeals.

Congress had ambitious goals when it gave the bureaucracy instructions to eliminate all discharges into the nation's waters by 1985, but numerous independent actors—among them the White House, the Justice Department, the media, industry, EPA's Research Office, outside contractors, and the courts—prevented this program from starting promptly and from being carried out without delay. Congress may authorize far-reaching goals, such as eliminating all discharges into the nation's waterways by 1985, but when autonomous actors have numerous opportunities to oppose these goals they are not likely to be achieved.

Notes

1. Federal Water Pollution Control Act Amendments of 1972, Public Law 92-5000, 70 Stat. 498; 84 Stat. 91, 33 U.S.C. 1151.

2. Best practicable technology was supposed to represent the "average of the best existing performance by well operated plants within each industrial category or subcategory." In industrial categories where existing treatment measures were generally inadequate, EPA had to set more stringent standards if the technology could be made available through good engineering

practice at a reasonable cost. Best available technology was supposed to be based upon the "very best control and treatment measures" that were capable of being economically achieved. The applications of the best available technology had to support two objectives: (1) achievement of the greatest amount of uniformity among categories of industries and (2) reduction in pollutants so that reasonable progress was being made to achieve the 1985 national goal of "no discharge."

3. "The President's Message on the Environment, February 10, 1970," reprinted in Council of Environmental Quality, *Environmental Quality: The First Annual Report* (Washington, D.C.: U.S. Government Printing Office, 1970), p. 259.

4. See United States Senate Committee on Public Works, *Water Pollution Control Legislation Hearings*, Parts 1, 2, and 3 (March 1971).

5. J. Clarence Davies and Barbara Davies, *The Politics of Pollution*, 2nd ed. (Indianapolis: Bobbs-Merrill, 1975), pp. 40-41.

6. Ibid., p. 42. Also see "The National Water Permit Program," pp. 4-26, "A Citizen's Guide to Clean Air" (Izaak Walton League, June 1973), and "Toward Cleaner Water: The New Permit Program to Control Water Pollution" (Washington, D.C.: EPA, January 1974).

7. Davies and Davies, *The Politics of Pollution*, p. 209.

8. See Richard S. Frank, "Environment Report/EPA and Justice Department Clash Over Anti-Pollution Enforcement," *National Journal Reports* (October 9, 1971), pp. 2048-53.

9. John Quarles, *Cleaning Up America* (Boston: Houghton Mifflin, 1976), p. 51.

10. Ibid.

11. Gladwin Hill, "New Penalty for Pollutors," *New York Times* (May 6, 1977), Section B, p. 9.

12. Rivers and Harbors Act of 1899, 33 U.S.C., Sections 403, 407, 411 (1899). See James R. Wagner, "Environment Report/Industries Win Few Concessions As Pollution Permit Plan Moves on Schedule," *National Journal Reports* (May 1, 1971), pp. 932-38; also see "The National Water Permit Program" (Washington, D.C.: EPA, June 1, 1973), pp. 1-4.

13. Quarles, *Cleaning Up America*, p. 103.

14. Ibid.

15. Ibid., p. 107.

16. Ibid., p. 110.

17. Ibid., p. 110.

18. Ibid., pp. 114. Also see Claude E. Barfield, "Environment Report/ Water Pollution Act Forces Showdown in 1973 Over Best Way to Protect Environment," *National Journal Report* (December 9, 1972), pp. 1871-82.

19. See "Effluent Limitations Guideline: Contractor Information" (Washington, D.C.: EPA, March 14, 1973). On the subject of contractors, see Daniel Guttman and Barry Willner, *The Shadow Government* (New York: Random House, 1976); also see Clarence H. Danhoff, *Government Contracting and Technological Change* (Washington, D.C.: The Brookings Institu-

tion, 1968); George Washington University, Federal Publications Incorporated, *Research and Development Contracting* (1963); and Bruce L. R. Smith, "Accountability and Independence in the Contract State," in *The Dilemma of Accountability in Modern Government,* ed. Bruce L. R. Smith and D. C. Hague (New York: St. Martin's Press, 1971).

20. See Arthur J. Magida, "Environment Report/EPA to Ask Congress to Relax Deadlines on Water Plan," *National Journal Reports* (December 21, 1974), pp. 1901-05.

21. See "Interim Effluent Guidance for NPDES Permits," (Washington, D.C.: EPA, May 1, 1973).

22. See Council on Environmental Quality, *The Environmental Quality: The Sixth Annual Report* (Washington, D.C.: U.S. Government Printing Office, 1975), pp. 60-68.

23. See CPC International Inc., et al., Petitioners *v.* Russell E. Train, et al., Respondents, *Brief for the Respondents on Remand* (U.S. Court of Appeals for the Eighth Circuit). Also see Development Document for Effluent Limitations Guidelines, *Grain Processing: Segment of the Grain Mills* (Washington, D.C.: EPA, March 1974). For a similar air pollution case, see Portland Cement Association, Petitioner *v.* Russell E. Train, Administrator, Environmental Protection Agency, Respondent, *Brief of Respondent Following Remand* (United States Circuit Court of Appeals for the District of Columbia Circuit).

7

Conclusion: Bureaucratic Performance and Divided Authority

The year 1977 marked the end of an era in EPA's history. In 1977 Congress passed new amendments to the 1970 Clean Air Act and 1972 Federal Water Pollution Control Act that thoroughly revised EPA's commitment to the original 1970 and 1972 pollution control goals and timetables.[1] Before 1977 and the passage of the new pollution control amendments, EPA achieved some of what Congress intended and some of what the White House intended, but while satisfying each branch partially, the agency satisfied neither completely.

Promise did not match performance. Congress delegated to the agency specific goals, but the means were altered and the goals were not achieved according to the schedule Congress established. The agency had a single environmental protection mission and an administrator chosen by the president, important innovations in regulatory administration, but it neither achieved its statutory goals in the timetable prescribed by Congress nor pursued these goals with regard to the least cost to society as the White House intended. If rationality is defined as the achievement of expected outcomes and the accomplishment of intended goals, then EPA achieved neither the expected outcomes nor the intended goals of the White House or of Congress.

The creation of EPA in 1970 and the passage of new pollution control statutes in 1970 and 1972 were innovations in regulatory policy in that the White House through structural change and Congress through statutory change tried to make the bureaucracy more accountable to the wishes of the two branches. These innovations in structure and statute brought into being not simple accountability to the White House and Congress but multiple accountability to a full range of institutions and groups. Bureaucratic performance, however, may not be compatible with accountability to a full range of institutions and groups in policymaking. EPA was constrained from achieving what the White House and Congress intended because power checked power so effectively that implementation was stifled and goals were not achieved.

Progress and Costs

EPA made some progress in cleaning the air and water, but it did not make the rapid and dramatic advances that Congress envisioned.[2] In 1975 almost 70 percent of the nation's 247 air quality control regions did not meet primary health standards. Nearly 20 percent of the industrial sources of air pollution had not complied with state implementation plan requirements. The noncomplying sources were major emitters, in particular utilities and steel mills that contributed most to the total emissions problem.[3] New car pollution, although it had been reduced substantially, did not meet the original 90 percent reduction requirement, and in 1977 nearly 10 percent of the nation's water pollutors had not installed best practicable technology according to the schedule established by Congress.

Evaluations of the costs of making this progress and its impact on the economy are uneven in quality. Cost studies are of questionable accuracy and reliability because economists use different methods of analysis. With these reservations in mind, the findings of a few studies will be noted. The Council of Environmental Quality estimated that pollution control cost each person living in the United States $47 in 1974 and $187 in 1977.[4] CEQ estimates showed that these costs would continue to rise to 2.5 percent of gross median family income before they started to decline again in the mid-1980s.

Robert Dorfman estimates that wealthy people have paid more for pollution control than poor people.[5] In 1976, he calculated that families with incomes over $11,410 paid on the average $549 a year for pollution control, while families earning less than $5,701 per year paid on the average $121 a year. At the same time, Dorfman argued that wealthy people generally have been willing to spend more for pollution control than poor people. Using a 1969 opinion survey about willingness to pay, he calculated that the wealthy were spending $59 *less* than they were willing to pay, while the poor were spending $61 *more* than they were willing to pay.

Macroeconomic studies have suggested that pollution control expenditures have contributed to some extent to unemployment and inflation.[6] Around 20,000 employees have lost their jobs because of plant closings, and the additional inflation attributable to pollution control was between .3 and .5 percent. In addition, industries, such as the electric utilities, faced severe capital shortages because of large pollution control expenditure requirements that have limited their capacity to grow.

Paul McCracken argued that these costs for pollution control will escalate greatly as the required amount of pollution reduction increases.[7] He maintained that the twenty-five-year costs to reach a 95 percent effluent reduction will be around $119 billion, while the cost of achieving the remaining reduction to achieve zero-discharge will be nearly $200 billion. The last five percentage points of reduction will be the most costly. Achieving zero-discharge will involve spending at least $81 billion more than achieving a 95 percent reduction.

These cost-evaluations, however, are not useful unless they are compared with pollution control benefits, but studies of pollution control benefits have been hard to come by because measuring benefits generally has been difficult.[8] The most sensitive problem is how to express in monetary terms the value of human life and health. In spite of this difficulty, some studies have estimated benefits and compared them with costs. In a study released in 1977, Lave and Seskin concluded that the benefits of controlling industrial smokestack emissions outweighed the costs, while the costs of controlling automobile emissions outweighed the benefits.[9] The "smokestack" emission's program, according to Lave and Seskin, would show a net benefit of $6.5 billion (in 1973 dollars), while the motor vehicle program would show a net loss of $6 billion (in 1973 dollars).[10]

The available studies suggest that EPA's impact on environmental quality and the nation's economy has been somewhere between what the White House wanted and the Congress was seeking. Although some progress had been made in cleaning the environment, neither congressional goals for rapid program achievement nor White House goals for minimizing the negative economic impact of pollution control have been achieved entirely. The agency's performance does not coincide completely with objectives established by Congress, and its achievements do not match precisely the expectations of the White House.

This result is not surprising given that public support for making sacrifices for the sake of pollution control has not been substantial. In 1970 and 1972 wealthier, better-educated segments of the public may have valued the health and recreational improvements that pollution control statutes promised but no segment of the public perceived that the main burden for cleaning the environment would fall on the shoulders of the average citizen. The common perception in 1970 and 1972 was that costs would be concentrated on specific industries and localities, while the average citizen would enjoy benefits.

Before the 1970 and 1972 pollution control acts were passed, benefits appeared to be diffused among the public at large and costs seemed to be concentrated on specific industries and localities; however, once these acts were implemented benefits that seemed intangible and distant had to be balanced against costs that appeared tangible and immediate. The motorist's immediate desire to get to work and to use his automobile without restrictions had to be balanced against the long-term and intangible costs of an unhealthy environment. When benefits appeared less tangible and more distant than the costs, the public was not willing to make significant sacrifices for the sake of pollution control. The improved health and recreational opportunities promised by the 1970 and 1972 acts did not appear to justify the immediate sacrifices.

The 1977 Amendments

In 1977, Congress substantially revised the earlier pollution control statutes. The new pollution control amendments modified, eliminated, and changed deadlines in the 1970 and 1972 pollution control laws in six ways.[11]

1. The 1977 air pollution amendments postponed the healthy air goals (that had to be achieved by 1975 under the 1970 act) to 1982 and in some instances to 1987. In areas heavily affected by auto emissions (e.g., California) the states had until 1987 to achieve air quality goals.
2. The 1977 air pollution amendments extended the deadline for 90 percent reductions in automobile emissions, originally set for 1975 and subsequently postponed to 1978, to 1980 for hydrocarbons and to 1981 for carbon monoxide. The administrator of EPA again was given discretionary authority to delay further the achievement of auto pollution reduction objectives, but only for carbon monoxide and nitrogen oxides, not for hydrocarbons. He could delay the 1981 carbon monoxide and nitrogen oxides standards for up to two years, if by taking into account factors, such as cost, driveability, fuel economy, and impacts on health, he determined that the required technology was not available.
3. The 1977 air pollution amendments required that EPA take into account competing priorities. It had to grant variances for technological innovation and file economic impact and employment impact statements with all new regulations it issued. In addition, the amendments gave the governor of any state the right to

suspend transportation control measures that required gas rationing, reductions in on-street parking, or bridge tolls.
4. The 1977 water pollution amendments also extended various deadlines. They gave industries that acted in "good faith," but did not meet the 1977 best practicable technology (BPT) deadlines, additional time to meet this standard. These industries had until April 1, 1979, instead of July 1, 1977.
5. The 1977 water pollution amendments also postponed and modified the best available technology (BAT) requirement that industry was supposed to achieve by 1983. They retained the strict standard for toxic pollutants but modified it for conventional pollutants. Conventional pollutants are solids, BOD (biochemical oxygen demanding pollutants), Ph, and fecal coliform. Instead of BAT, BCPCT—best conventional pollution control technology—had to be achieved. According to the Conference Committee, BCPCT was at least as stringent as best practicable technology, but not more stringent than best available technology. BCPCT gave EPA flexibility to set standards less stringent than BAT when the costs of employing BAT exceeded benefits. Industrial discharges now had to meet BCPCT by 1984 instead of BAT by 1983.
6. The 1977 amendments retained the goal of zero-discharge into navigable waters by 1985, but the practical implications of retaining this goal were few. The extension of the BPT objective and the modification of the BAT objective eliminated the connection between zero-discharge and a specific abatement program. The 1977 amendments, while not directly changing the zero-discharge goal, effectively abandoned it for the 1970s [12]

The 1977 amendments, while harmonizing to some extent legislative and executive goals, extended most of EPA's deadlines. Exceptions, conditions, and specific categories in these amendments gave EPA the authority to put off achievement of its original air and water pollution objectives. The passage of these amendments have set a precedent for delay. It becomes reasonable to expect that timetables once delayed are capable of being delayed again; and deadlines that are delayed lose much of their credibility.

The 1977 amendments signified a reduction in the conflict between congressional goals and White House ambitions.

Under the 1977 amendments, EPA had to take into account the economic cost of new air and water pollution regulations. If the administrator granted the auto companies another extension, fuel economy and economic implications had to be explicitly considered. These cost and energy related revisions of the original 1970 and 1972 acts implied a greater national consensus about the role of environmental objectives and their relation to other national priorities.

After these revisions were made, however, one could discern a new pattern of conflict emerging between bureaucrats, who had a policy perspective and were more closely connected to the White House and its national economic and energy goals, and bureaucrats, who had a program perspective and were more closely tied to Congress and its specific pollution control goals. This conflict, not limited by particular political party or administration, appears to be a constant in environmental policymaking.

Three Approaches to Pollution Control

Congress could have taken three approaches when it drafted the 1977 amendments.[13] It could have drafted vague legislation with general goals but not specific instructions as to how or when to achieve these goals as it did in the case of the older regulatory commissions. A second alternative would have been for Congress to continue to rely upon clear statutes with specific goals, timetables, and instructions, which essentially it did. However, there is a third method of controlling pollution which has not been tried on a widespread basis that Congress could have used. Congress could have adopted a market or incentive approach which did not have deadlines and was not oriented toward the achievement of particular goals by specific dates.

The market or incentive approach, widely celebrated in economic literature, decentralizes decision-making. It relies upon individual firms that possess the information needed for making optimum cost-benefit and efficiency trade-offs. It is a more direct way to control pollution, because it eliminates steps involving numerous actors, decisions, and clearances that bring about delay. Individual decisions in response to market incentives would lead to choices between environmental control, energy use, and economic growth which EPA found so difficult to make. The "hidden hand" of the market, not the "heavy hand" of the bureaucracy, would allocate resources among competing ends. If there is a dominant innovative idea about regulation that academics, particularly economists, promote today it is the notion that the market or incentive approach is superior to other other approaches.

The 1977 amendments, by creating a limited market for emission rights in non-attainment areas, introduced a version of a market or incentive method.[14] In 1976, EPA began to allow growth of new pollution sources in non-attainment regions, if deterioration in air quality caused by the sources was more than offset by emission reduction in other facilities. For example, EPA was going to allow Standard Oil of Ohio (SOHIO) to build a pipeline terminal near Long Beach, California, after SOHIO bought another nearby polluting facility and closed it down. Under the 1977 amendments, EPA obtained authority to set up a limited market for trading in emission rights in non-attainment areas. This market existed under the 1977 amendments until 1979. In 1979 attainment areas without state implementation plans that ensure attainment of air quality objectives by 1982 faced a ban on new sources of emission. In effect, their industrial growth was restricted.

The offset policy was not a major breakthrough in the use of a market or incentive approach. Under the 1977 amendments, EPA's authority to use this method was limited. When Congress drafted the 1977 amendments, it considered pollution tax and effluent charge schemes the most commonly discussed market or incentive systems.[15] The 1977 amendments, however, did not adopt these schemes. Instead a penalty provision in the 1970 Clean Air Act was changed. A firm no longer could avoid paying for the costs of pollution control by court delays.[16] Under the 1977 amendments, the violating firm could be assessed a fine equivalent to the amount it could save by judicial delay.

Market or incentive schemes were not adopted mostly because they encountered political obstacles: the opposition of Senator Muskie, Treasury Department officials and powerful members of Congress, industry, and environmentalists. Lacking strong support from any group and without significant support from the public or leadership from the White House, effluent charge and pollution tax proposals were doomed politically.[17] EPA continued to rely mainly on timetables and standards. Deadlines were delayed, but not eliminated. The 1977 amendments brought EPA closer to a vague "let the bureaucracy decide" method. It grafted economic incentives in an incremental and piecemeal fashion on an existing directive framework. It qualified but it did not eliminate the basic goal and timetable approach.

Deviations from Rational Models

Very few programs act in accord with rational models. The purpose of a comparison between rational models and actual behavior is not to make final judgments about program performance. The purpose, in this instance, is to give prominence to how EPA actually chose and implemented environmental policy and to develop alternative models of policy choice and policy implementation.

Rational models assume single-minded decision-making and single-minded implementation—control from above, from a single policymaking source that gives instructions—and compliance from below, from a united bureaucracy that receives and carries out these instructions.[18] With respect to implementation they assume a united bureaucracy with a single will that receives without distortion or confusion instructions communicated with clarity and consistency by a single decision maker. This bureaucracy, even when it is in a rapidly changing environment in which there is pervasive conflict among competing interests, is able to coordinate complex action that involves many participants and decisions. It is predictable in its achievement of outcomes, and it maximizes intended outcomes and minimizes unintended outcomes within a limited time period.

Rational models of policy choice and policy implementation assume intentional, designed, and purposeful action. They assume that policy is made by a single entity that poses and solves problems and that policy is implemented by a united bureaucracy that receives instructions without deviation and carries them out without delay.

In the choosing and implementing of environmental policy the government did not operate in accord with rational models. Decision-making was not by a single decision maker but by two authoritative bodies, the White House, which created EPA, and Congress, which passed important pollution control statutes. These parties had diverse goals and intentions. They made no effort to coordinate their actions or work as a unit. They did not function as a collective mind that carefully defined a problem, enumerated alternatives, considered consequences, and gave a uniform set of instructions to the bureaucracy. On the contrary, they presented dual and conflicting instructions to the EPA.

Each policymaking source started by considering different proposals. Instead of a single, goal-maximizing decision maker, detached from political involvements, policy was decided by two decision makers operating in different political arenas and subject to the influence of different groups and pressures.

The administrator of the new agency and the bureaucrats he inherited responded to two sets of instructions. Discretionary behavior by the administrator and by EPA bureaucrats was possible because of divided decision-making. Ambiguity about what was supposed to be done prevented EPA's bureaucrats from closely following the commands they received from either Congress or the White House.

The problem of complexity of joint action is summarized in Tables 13 and 14. Institutions and groups reflecting a large and heterogenous society played a role in carrying out EPA's

TABLE 13
The Complexity of Joint Action: Carrying out the 1970 Clean Air Act*

Decision Points Participants	A. The Cost of Pollution Control: The first auto pollution extension	B. The Energy Crisis: The second auto pollution extension	C. "Acid Emissions": The third auto pollution extension	D. The Imposition of Transportation Control
General public	X	X	X	X
Media		X	X	
White House (including the Office of Management and Budget and the president)	X			
Commerce Department	X			
Congress (with special reference to Senate Pollution Control Committee)	X	X		X
Courts	X			X
EPA				
Ruckelshaus	X			X
Train			X	
Researchers in North Carolina			X	
Staff in Washington and Ann Arbor			X	
Regional offices				X

*X in the box denotes significant involvement in the decision. Refer to Chapter 5 for details of the participants' involvement.

	A	B	C	D
Environmentalists (National Resources Defense Council)				X
Industry				
Auto manufacturers as a unit	X	X		
Utilities		X		
Ford Motor Company			X	
Catalyst manufacturers			X	
Outside sources of information				
National Academy of Sciences	X	X		
Contractors and consulting firms			X	X
Local politicians, governments, and citizens				
California Air Resources Board			X	
Municipalities of Riverside and San Bernadino				X
Businesses				X
Construction unions				X
Taxi drivers				X

statutes. The Senate and the House had a different view of how the zero-discharge provision of the 1972 Federal Water Pollution Control Act should be carried out. The Ford Motor Company, the catalyst manufacturers, and General Motors had different views of what should be done about auto pollution deadlines. Local participants sued to have transportation control measures imposed, while other local actors vigorously opposed their imposition.

Conflict also existed within the bureaucracy. Research scientists in North Carolina interpreted the threat of acid emissions differently from EPA's air pollution staff in Washington and Ann Arbor. Similarly, in the issuing of effluent guidelines, the Enforcement Office proceeded at a more rapid pace than the Effluent Guidelines Division. The courts also were divided. Their interpretation of the law involved using different principles for different cases. The courts, for instance, forced Ruckelshaus to reconsider his denial of the auto companies' request for an extension of the original 90 percent reduction in five years. They then compelled Ruckelshaus to impose unpopular transportation control requirements.

In choosing and implementing an environmental policy there was neither single-minded decision-making nor single-minded implementation—neither control from above by a single policymaking source that gave bureaucrats a single set of instructions nor compliance from below from a united bureaucracy that received and carried out these instructions. Deviations from rational models occurred because of the existence of autonomous actors and no one with the power or authority to concert their actions. Dual instructions and a divided bureaucracy led to a situation where power effectively counteracted power in the actual carrying out of policy.

An Experiment in Regulatory Reform

EPA is one of the few regulatory agencies where a single administrator, not a group of commissioners, manages the agency. It is one of the few that has independent status and is not lodged in the bottom of another department. Similarly, its statutes were composed in such a way that the agency has explicit authority from Congress to achieve specific goals by definite dates. In its structure and in its statutes, the agency is an experiment in regulatory reform, an experiment

TABLE 14
The Complexity of Joint Action: Carrying Out the 1972 Federal Water Pollution Control Act*

Decision Points / Participants	A. The Passage of 1972 FWPCA	B. Interim Strategies		C. Issuing Effluent Guidelines
		1. Suits	2. Permits	
Media		X		
White House	X		X	
Congress				
Senate Pollution Control Subcommittee	X			
Representative Henry Reuss			X	
House Public Works Committee	X			
Conference Committee	X			
Courts		X		X
Justice Department attorneys		X		
Commerce Department economists			X	
Army Corps of Engineers			X	
EPA				
Acting Administrator Fri				X
Enforcement Office		X		X
Effluent Guidelines Division				X
Regional offices		X		

*X in the column denotes significant involvement in the decision.
Refer to Chapter 6 for details of the participants' involvement.

	A	B	C
Industry			
Company attorneys	X	X	X
Trade associations		X	X
Environmentalists (National Resources Defense Council)		X	
Outside sources of information			
Contractors		X	X
Professional associations			X
States and localities	X		

designed to increase EPA's accountability to the White House and Congress. Increased accountability to these constitutionally sanctioned authorities, however, is not the same as increased rationality. If bureaucratic performance were synonymous with rational action—with the achievement of intended outcomes within specified time periods— then this experiment in regulatory reform would not be a success. Bureaucratic performance, however, has a broader meaning. Other values besides rationality have to be considered. If other values are considered, it is possible to compare the advantages and disadvantages of divided authority with the advantages and disadvantages of concentrated authority.

ADVANTAGES OF DIVIDED AUTHORITY

(1) Lack of coercion. Because power checks power and no single power dominates, relevant interests are more likely to have access to government and to be satisfied.

(2) Many minds interacting. Because of the diversity of potential actors, participants become watchdogs for values

neglected by others. They become sensitive to certain lines of consequences and more competent to explore them than others for whom these consequences are incidental.[19]

(3) Flexibility. Bureaucrats are less likely to accept orders passively and carry out the commands they receive no matter what the consequences. They are more likely to alter their behavior in response to situations they actually face.

(4) Reliability. Bureaucrats have more of a chance to correct errors as they proceed. The "redundancy" of command and authority makes the system more reliable.[20]

DISADVANTAGES OF DIVIDED AUTHORITY

(1) Uncertainty of outcome. Because there is no "visible hand" that guides action, delays are possible and goals may not be achieved.[21]

(2) Slowness of change. A portion of the public is likely to become dissatisfied with the slow pace of change. Given the apparent disorder, public confidence in the ability of the state to perform what it sets out to accomplish may be harder to sustain.

(3) Wastefulness. If hesitant starts and sudden stops could be reduced, resources could be concentrated on achieving specific goals within intended time periods.

THE ADVANTAGES OF CONCENTRATED AUTHORITY

(1) Doing what is "right." The premise of concentrating authority is not that policymakers force policy implementors to do what they have been told, but that impersonal orders are issued so that the bureaucracy can accomplish "what is right."[22] Explicit decision-making criteria can be used in making choices, and what is done will be based on reason, not mere agreement.

(2) Systematic pursuit of objectives. Guided by reasonably chosen objectives bureaucrats should act in support of each other's actions to insure that outputs are based on a knowledge of inputs and are therefore predictable.

(3) Stable expectations. The probability that intended objectives will result in expected outcomes should increase. The populace, therefore, should be able to have confidence that when government promises, it performs, that when it establishes goals, it attains them.

(4) The possibility of rapid change. If the government indicates that by certain dates, it will produce certain results, these changes are more likely to occur. Major change is more likely to happen.

THE DISADVANTAGES OF CONCENTRATED AUTHORITY

(1) Costliness of maintaining control. If what is promulgated by the authority is not accepted as being "right," then coercive measures may be necessary to maintain control.[23] Diverse opinions would have to be suppressed and dissenting groups contained.

(2) Rigidity. The bureaucracy, coerced to carry out a policy, would not investigate errors and make independent corrective judgments. New factors could emerge to undercut commitment to original goals, but policymakers would not obtain the information to respond adequately and make the necessary changes.

(3) Likelihood of error. Error is likely if policymakers lose touch with changing circumstances and conditions. The failure of a single part of the system could set off a chain reaction that would result in major problems.[24]

EPA enjoyed the advantages of divided authority. It tended to be noncoercive, open to diverse groups and opinions, flexible, and cautious. But it suffered the disadvantages. It also tended to be unpredictable in terms of outcome, slow in bringing about change, and wasteful of taxpayers' resources. Had it been subject to concentrated authority, it is likely that it would have pursued objectives more systematically, maximized achievement of expected outcomes, and made more rapid environmental improvement. But these gains only could have been won at a price—the price of coercive power, rigidity, and nonattention to changing circumstances.

In choosing and implementing an environmental policy, divided authority may have been appropriate. In a situation where benefits that appeared distant and intangible had to be balanced against costs that seemed immediate and tangible, there were grounds for legitimate differences of opinion. Some may have been willing to accept the burden of immediate, tangible sacrifices for the sake of distant, intangible benefits, but others had legitimate reasons for preferring to avoid immediate sacrifices for the sake of distant non-material ends. When tangible and immediate costs have to be balanced against intangible and distant benefits, it may be appropriate for the government to accommodate a broad range of groups and opinions and to be accountable to many actors.

However, it is possible to imagine situations where strict conformity to this pluralistic pattern would be questionable. If benefits were perceived as immediate and tangible and costs also were perceived as immediate and tangible and there was a "crisis" where delay would mean that costs would far outweigh benefits, the government would have more reason to respond with single-minded intention and action. Environmental problems may be divided into two categories: (1) those like air and water pollution control where health and recreational benefits that seem distant and intangible have to be balanced against immediate and tangible costs, and delay would be acceptable because immediate costs would not outweigh immediate benefits; and (2) those like toxic substances or nuclear safety where both the costs and benefits of choosing and implementing a policy are tangible and immediate and delay could be intolerable. The former group can be appropriately handled within the confines of a pluralistic system, while the latter group may require greater certainty about what path to follow and greater control from above once a correct path has been chosen.

Notes

1. Clean Air Amendments of 1977, Pub. L. No. 95-99, 91 Stat. 685 (1977) and Clean Water Act of 1977. Pub. L. No. 95-217, 91 Stat. 1566-1611 (1977).

2. The statistics on EPA's progress in achieving congressional objectives can be found in Council on Environmental Quality, *Environmental Quality: The Sixth Annual Report* (Washington, D.C.: U.S. Government Printing Office, 1975).

3. See Alfred Marcus, "Command and Control": An Assessment of Smokestack Emission Regulation," working paper (Pittsburgh: University of Pittsburgh, Graduate School of Business, 1978).

4. *Environmental Quality: The Sixth Annual Report*, p. 533 and Council on Environmental Quality, *Environmental Quality: The Eighth Annual Report* (Washington, D.C.: U.S. Government Printing Office, 1977), p. 323.

5. Robert Dorfman, "Benefits and Costs of Environmental Programs" *Society* (March/April 1977), pp. 63-66. Also see Nancy Dorfman and Arthur Snow, "Who Will Pay for Pollution Control?" *National Tax Journal* 28 (March 1975) pp. 101-15.

6. *Environmental Quality: The Sixth Annual Report*, pp. 533-544. *Environmental Quality: The Eighth Annual Report* estimates that there were 677,900 people employed directly for pollution abatement in 1974, see p. 332.

7. Paul McCracken, chairman, Council of Economic Advisers, Russell Train, chairman, CEQ, and William Ruckelshaus, administrator, EPA, in remarks about the Senate bill before the House Public Works Committee, *Hearings on H. R. 11896, H.R. 11895 to Amend the Federal Water Pollution Control Act* (Washington, D.C.: U. S. Government Printing Office, December 7, 1971), p. 213.

8. See *Environmental Quality: The Eighth Annual Report.* CEQ in 1977 decided not to include benefit studies in its discussion of environmental economics.

9. Lester Lave and Eugene Seskin, *The Costs and Benefits of Air Pollution Control* (Washington D.C.: Resources for the Future, 1977). Their findings can be contrasted with an earlier NAS study that concluded that the cost to achieve motor vehicle standards would be between $5 billion and $11 billion while the benefits would be between $3.6 billion and $14.3 billion. National Academy of Sciences, *Air Quality and Automobile Emission Control, the Cost and Benefits of Automobile Emission Control—A Report by the Coordinating Committee on Air Quality Studies*, vol. 4, prepared for the Committee on Public Works, U. S. Senate, pursuant to S. Res. 135, approved August 3, 1973 (Washington, D.C.: U. S. Government Printing Office, 1974), p. 78, Tables 2-14 and p. 417, Tables 6-7.

10. Lester Lave and Eugene Seskin, *The Costs and Benefits of Air Pollution Control* (Washington, D.C.: Resources for the Future, 1977).

11. This account of the 1977 amendments is derived primarily from Christopher Davis, Jeffrey Kurtok, James P. Leape, and Frank Magill, "The Clean Air Act Amendments of 1977: Away from Technology Forcing?" *Harvard Environmental Law Review* 2 (1977), pp. 1-103 and James Voytko, Kurt M. Hunaker, and Richard Lazarus, "The Clean Water Act and Related Developments in the Federal Water Pollution Control Program During 1977," *Harvard Environmental Law Review* 2 (1977), pp. 103-199. See also *Environmental Quality: The Eighth Annual Report*, pp. 22-27 and Edmund

Muskie, "The Meaning of the 1977 Clean Water Act" *EPA Journal*, 4 (July/August 1978), pp. 4, 36.

12. See Voytko, et al., pp. 126, 125. See Bernard Asbell, "The Outlawing of Next Year's Cars," *The New York Times Magazine* (November 21, 1976), p. 41.

13. See Barry M. Mitnick, "Organizing Regulation: Consideration in Regulation by Incentive and by Directive," working paper (College of Administrative Sciences, The Ohio State University, March 1977).

14. See Bruce Yandle, "The Emerging Market in Air Pollution Rights," *Regulation* (July/August 1978), pp. 21-30.

15. Charles L. Schultze, "The Public Use of Private Interest," *Regulation* (Sept./Oct. 1977), pp. 10-14. Also see Allen V. Kneese and Charles L. Schultze, *Pollution, Prices and Public Policy* (Washington, D.C.: The Brookings Institution, 1975) or Larry S. Ruff, "The Economic Common Sense of Pollution," *The Public Interest* (Spring 1970), pp. 69-85. Ruff's article and many others on tax and charge systems to reduce pollution are contained in a congressional report. See the Environment and Natural Resources Policy divisions of the Congressional Research Service, *Pollution Taxes, Effluent Charges, and Other Alternatives for Pollution Control* (U. S. Senate Committee on Environment and Public Works, 1977). This 869-page collection of articles, probably the most comprehensive ever assembled on the subject of incentives, pollution taxes, effluent charges, and other alternatives consisted of 835 pages devoted to a discussion of incentives, charges, and pollution taxes and 34 pages devoted to sanctions and penalties.

16. The new penalty provision is called "The Connecticut Plan" because it was first tried in the state of Connecticut when present EPA administrator Douglas Costle was director of environmental affairs in that state. For a technical discussion of this penalty provision, its origin and how it will function see Davis, Kurtock, et al., pp. 78-83. See also A. Michael Spence and Martin L. Weitzman, "Regulatory Strategies for Pollution Control" especially the comments by William Drayton, Jr., in *Approaches to Controlling Air Pollution,* ed. Ann F. Friedlaender (Cambridge, Mass.: MIT Press, 1978), pp. 199-240.

17. James E. Anderson, David W. Brady, and Charles Bullock, III, *Public Policy and Politics in America* (North Scituate, Mass.: Duxbury Press, 1978), p. 89.

18. See Max Weber, "Essay on Bureaucracy" in *From Max Weber: Essay in Sociology,* ed. H. Gerth and C. Wright Mills (New York: Oxford University Press, 1946), pp. 196-235.

19. See "Between Planning and Politics: Intellect vs. Interaction as Analysis" in Aaron Wildavsky, *Speaking Truth to Power: The Art and Craft of Policy Analysis* (Boston: Little Brown and Company, 1979), pp. 114-42.

20. See Martin Landau, "Redundancy, Rationality and the Problem of Duplication and Overlap" *Public Administration Review* (July/August 1969), pp. 346-58.

21. See Theodore Lowi, *The End of Liberalism* (New York: W. W. Norton, 1969).

22. See Mary Parker Follet, "The Giving of Orders" in *Classics of Public Administration* ed. Jay Shafritz and Albert C. Hyde (Oak Park, Ill.: Moore Publishing Co., 1978), pp. 29-37.

23. See Kenneth Arrow, *The Limits of Organization* (New York: W. W. Norton, 1974).

24. See Landau, "Redundancy, Rationality."

Bibliography

Policymaking and Implementation

Allison, Graham T. *Essence of Decision.* Boston: Little, Brown, 1971.

Anderson, James E., ed. *Cases in Public Policy-Making.* New York: Praeger, 1976.

Anderson, James E., David W. Brady, and Charles Bullock III. *Public Policy and Politics in America.* North Scituate, Mass.: Duxbury Press, 1978.

Backoff, Robert. "Operationalizing Administrative Reform for Improved Governmental Performance." *Administration and Society* 6 (May 1974):73-106.

Bailey, Stephen K. *The New Congress.* New York: St. Martin's Press, 1966.

Banfield, Edward C. *Political Influence.* New York: Free Press, 1961.

Banfield, Edward C., and James Q. Wilson. *City Politics.* Cambridge, Mass.: Harvard University Press and M.I.T. Press, 1963.

Bardach, Eugene. *The Implementation Game: What Happens After a Bill Becomes a Law.* Cambridge, Mass.: M.I.T. Press, 1977.

Bauer, Raymond, and Kenneth Gergen, eds. *The Study of Policy Formation.* New York: Free Press, 1968.

Bauer, Raymond, Ithiel Pool, and Lewis Dexter. *American Business and Public Policy.* New York: Atherton Press, 1963.

Berman, Paul. "The Study of Macro- and Micro-Implementation." *Public Policy* 26 (Spring 1978):157-185.

Berry, Jeffrey M. *Lobbying for the People.* Princeton, N.J.: Princeton University Press, 1977.

Blechman, Barry M., Edward M. Gramlich, and Robert W. Hartman. *Setting National Priorities: The 1976 Budget.* Washington, D.C.: Brookings Institution, 1975.

Braybrooke, David, and Charles E. Lindblom. *Strategy of Decision: Policy Evaluation as a Social Process.* New York: Free Press, 1970.

Clapp, Charles L. *The Congressman—His Work As He Sees It.* Garden City, N. Y.: Anchor Books, Doubleday, 1963.

Cobb, Roger, and Charles Elder. *Participation in American Politics: The Dynamics of Agenda-Building.* Baltimore: Johns Hopkins University Press, 1972.

Cronin, Thomas E. *The State of the Presidency.* Boston: Little, Brown, 1975.

Dahl, Robert A., and Charles E. Lindblom. *Politics, Economics, and*

185

Welfare. Chicago: University of Chicago Press, 1976.

Davis, Morton. *Game Theory.* New York: Basic Books, 1973.

Diesing, Paul. *Patterns of Discovery in the Social Sciences.* Chicago: Aldine, 1971.

Dodd, Lawrence C., and Bruce I. Oppenheimer. *Congress Reconsidered.* New York: Praeger, 1977.

Dolbeare, Kenneth, ed. *Public Policy Evaluation.* Beverly Hills, Calif.: Sage Publications, 1975.

Dror, Yehezkel. *Public Policy Reexamined.* San Francisco: Chandler, 1968.

Dye, Thomas R. *Understanding Public Policy.* Englewood Cliffs, N.J.: Prentice-Hall, 1978.

Eckstein, Otto. *Public Finance.* Englewood Cliffs, N.J.: Prentice-Hall, 1979.

Edelman, Murray. *The Symbolic Uses of Politics.* Urbana, Ill.: University of Illinois Press, 1964.

Edwards, George C., and Ira Sharkansky. *The Policy Predicament: Making and Implementing Public Policy.* San Francisco: W.H. Freeman, 1978.

Eisenstein, James. *Politics and the Legal Process.* New York: Harper & Row, 1973.

Elmore, Richard. "Organizational Models of Social Program Implementation." *Public Policy* 26 (Spring 1978):185-229.

Enthoven, Alain C., and K. Wayne Smith. *How Much Is Enough? Shaping the Defense Program.* New York: Harper Colophon Books, 1971.

Etzioni, Amitai. "Mixed Scanning: A 'Third' Approach to Decision Making." *Public Administration Review* 27 (December 1967):385-392.

Gutman, Daniel, and Barry Wilner. *The Shadow Government.* New York: Pantheon Books, 1976.

Halper, Thomas. *Foreign Policy Crises.* Columbus, Ohio: Charles E. Merrill, 1971.

Hamilton, Alexander, James Madison, and John Jay. *The Federalist Papers.* New York: New American Library, 1961.

Hargrove, Erwin. "Implementation." *Policy Studies Journal* 5 (Autumn 1976):9-15.

Hawley, Willis D., and Frederick M. Wirt, eds. *The Search for Community Power.* Englewood Cliffs, N.J.: Prentice-Hall, 1968.

Heidenheimer, Arnold J., Hugh Heclo, and Carolyn Terch Adams. *Comparative Public Policy: The Politics of Social Choice in Europe and America.* New York: St. Martin's Press, 1975.

Hoover, Kenneth R. *The Elements of Social Scientific Thinking.* New York: St. Martin's Press, 1976.

Jones, Charles O. *An Introduction to the Study of Public Policy.* Belmont, Calif.: Duxbury Press, 1970.

_____. "Why Congress Can't Do Policy Analysis (or Words to That Effect)." *Policy Analysis* 2 (Spring 1976):251-263.

Jones, Charles O., and Robert D. Thomas, eds. *Public Policy Making in a Federal System.* Beverly Hills, Calif.: Sage Publications, 1976.

Kariel, Henry S. *The Decline of American Pluralism*. Stanford, Calif.: Stanford University Press, 1961.

Labovitz, Sanford, and Robert Hagedorn. *Introduction to Social Research*. New York: McGraw-Hill, 1976.

Larson, James. "When Government Programs Fail." Paper prepared for delivery at the 1978 annual meeting of the American Political Science Association.

Lazard, Richard, ed. *Cost-Benefit Analysis*. New York: Penguin, 1974.

Lazarus, Simon. *The Genteel Populists*. New York: Holt, Rinehart & Winston, 1974.

Lerner, Daniel, and Harold D. Lasswell, eds. *The Policy Sciences*. Stanford, Calif.: Stanford University Press, 1951.

Levi, Edward L. *An Introduction to Legal Reasoning*. Chicago: University of Chicago Press, 1949.

Lewin, Arie Y., and Melvin F. Shakun. *Policy Sciences*. New York: Pergamon Press, 1976.

Lindblom, Charles E. *The Policy-Making Process*. Englewood Cliffs, N.J.: Prentice-Hall, 1968.

———. "The Science of Muddling Through." *Public Administration Review* 19 (Spring 1959):79-88.

Lowi, Theodore. *The End of Liberalism*. New York: Norton, 1979.

Lowi, Theodore, and Alan Stare, eds. *Nationalizing Government Public Policies in America*. Beverly Hills, Calif.: Sage Publications, 1978.

McConnell, Grant. *The Modern Presidency*. New York: St. Martin's Press, 1976.

McFarland, Andrew S. *Public Interest Lobbies: Decision Making on Energy*. Washington, D.C.: American Enterprise Institute, 1976.

Mahood, H. R., ed. *Pressure Groups in American Politics*. New York: Charles Scribner's Sons, 1957.

Marcus, Alfred A. "Public Interest Leaders: Whom Do They Represent?" *Business Horizons* 22 (August 1979):84-88.

May, Judith V., and Aaron B. Wildavsky, eds. *The Policy Cycle*. Beverly Hills, Calif.: Sage Publications, 1978.

Meltsner, Arnold J. *Policy Analysts in the Bureaucracy*. Berkeley: University of California Press, 1976.

Mintzberg, Henry, Duru Raismghani, and Andre Théorèt. "The Structure of 'Unstructured' Decision Processes." *Administrative Science Quarterly* 21 (June 1976):246-275.

Mitnick, Barry. "A Typology of Conceptions of the Public Interest." *Administration and Society* 8 (May 1976):5-28.

Moore, P. G., and H. Thomas, eds. *The Anatomy of Decisions*. New York: Penguin Books, 1976.

Mosher, Frederick C., and Richard J. Stillman II, eds. "A Symposium: The Professions in Government II." *Public Administration Review* (March/April 1978):105-125.

Moynihan, Daniel. *Maximum Feasible Misunderstanding*. New York: Free Press, 1970.

Myerson, M., and E. C. Banfield. *Politics, Planning and the Public Interest.* New York: Free Press, 1955.

Nachmias, David. *Public Policy Evaluation: Approaches and Methods.* New York: St. Martin's Press, 1979.

Nathan, Richard P. *The Plot That Failed: Nixon and the Administrative Presidency.* New York: John Wiley & Sons, 1975.

Neustadt, Richard E. *Presidential Power.* New York: John Wiley & Sons, 1976.

Orfield, Gary. *Congressional Power: Congress and Social Change.* New York: Harcourt, Brace & Jovanovich, 1975.

Owen, Henry, and Charles L. Schultze, eds. *Setting National Priorities: The Next Ten Years.* Washington, D.C.: Brookings Institution, 1976.

Pechman, Joseph A., ed. *Setting National Priorities: The 1978 Budget.* Washington, D.C.: Brookings Institution, 1977.

Piven, Frances Fox, and Richard A. Cloward. *Regulating the Poor.* New York: Random House, 1971.

Pogue, Thomas F., and L. G. Sgontz. *Government and Economic Choice.* Boston: Houghton Mifflin, 1978.

Pressman, Jeffrey L., and Aaron B. Wildavsky. *Implementation: How Great Expectations in Washington Are Dashed in Oakland.* Berkeley: University of California Press, 1974.

Price, Don K. *The Scientific Estate.* Cambridge, Mass.: Harvard University Press, 1965.

Quade, E. S. *Analysis for Public Decision.* New York: Elsevier North-Holland, 1978.

Rabinovitz, Francine, Jeffrey Pressman, and Martin Rein. "Guidelines: A Plethora of Forms, Authors, and Functions." *Policy Sciences* 7 (1976):399-416.

Raiffa, Howard. *Decision Analysis.* Reading, Mass.: Addison-Wesley, 1970.

Rawls, John. *A Theory of Justice.* Cambridge, Mass.: Harvard University Press, 1971.

Rothman, Jack. *Planning and Organizing for Social Change.* New York: Columbia University Press, 1974.

Scharansky, Ira, ed. *Policy Analysis in Political Service.* Chicago: Markham, 1977.

Schattschneider, E. E. *The Semi-Sovereign People.* New York: Holt, Rinehart & Winston, 1960.

Schilling, Thomas C. *The Strategy of Conflict.* London: Oxford University Press, 1960.

Schlesinger, Arthur M. *The Imperial Presidency.* Boston: Houghton Mifflin, 1973.

Shor, Edgar, ed. "A Symposium: Public Interest Representation and the Federal Agencies." *Public Administration Review* (March/April 1977):131-154.

Simon, Julian. *Basic Research Methods in Social Science.* New York: Random House, 1978.

Steinbruner, John D. *The Cybernetic Theory of Decision.* Princeton, N.J.: Princeton University Press, 1974.

Stokey, Edith, and Richard Zeckhauser. *A Primer for Policy Analysis.* New York: W. W. Norton, 1978.

Sundquist, James L. *Politics and Policy: The Eisenhower, Kennedy, and Johnson Years.* Washington, D.C.: Brookings Institution, 1971.

Tripodi, Tony, Phillip Fellin, and Irwin Epstein. *Social Program Evaluation.* Itasca, Ill.: F. E. Peacock, 1971.

Tropman, John E., Milan Dluhy, Roger Lind, Wayne Vasey, and Tom A. Croxton, eds. *Strategic Perspectives on Social Policy.* New York: Pergamon Press, 1976.

Truman, David, ed. *The Congress and America's Future.* Englewood Cliffs, N.J.: Prentice-Hall, 1973.

_____. *The Governmental Process.* New York: Alfred A. Knopf, 1971.

Tufte, Edward R. *Data Analysis for Politics and Policy.* Englewood Cliffs, N.J.: Prentice-Hall, 1974.

Van Meter, Donald S., and Carl E. Van Horn. "The Policy Implementation Process." *Administration and Society* 6 (February 1975):445-487.

Vogel, David. "Promoting Pluralism: The Public Interest Movement and the American Reform Tradition." Paper prepared for delivery at the 1978 annual meeting of the American Political Science Association.

Weiss, Carol. *Evaluation Research.* Englewood Cliffs, N.J.: Prentice-Hall, 1972.

Wildavsky, Aaron. *The Politics of the Budgetary Process.* Boston: Little, Brown, 1964.

_____. *Speaking Truth to Power: The Art and Craft of Policy Analysis.* Boston: Little, Brown, 1979.

Wilson, James Q. "American Politics: Then and Now." *Commentary* (February 1979):39-46.

_____. *Political Organizations.* New York: Basic Books, 1973.

_____. *Thinking About Crime.* New York: Random House, 1975.

Woll, Peter. *Public Policy.* Cambridge, Mass.: Winthrop, 1974.

Zisk, Betty, ed. *American Political Interest Groups.* Belmont, Calif.: Wadsworth, 1969.

Organization and Administration

Altshuler, Alan A., and Norman C. Thomas. *The Politics of the Federal Bureaucracy.* New York: Harper & Row, 1977.

Arrow, Kenneth J. *The Limits of Organization.* New York: Norton, 1974.

Balzano, Michael P. *Reorganizing the Federal Bureaucracy: The Rhetoric and the Reality.* Washington, D.C.: American Enterprise Institute, 1977.

Barnard, Chester I. *The Functions of the Executive.* Cambridge, Mass.: Harvard University Press, 1968.

Benveniste, Guy. *Bureaucracy.* San Francisco: Boyd and Fraser, 1977.
———. *The Politics of Expertise.* San Francisco: Boyd and Fraser, 1977.
Blau, Peter M. *The Dynamics of Bureaucracy.* Chicago: University of Chicago Press, 1963.
Bower, Joseph, and Charles Christenson. *Public Management: Text and Cases.* Homewood, Ill.: Richard Irwin, 1978.
Chandler, Alfred D. *Strategy and Structure.* Cambridge, Mass.: M.I.T. Press, 1962.
Crozier, Michel. *The Bureaucratic Phenomenon.* Chicago: University of Chicago Press, 1964.
Cyert, Richard, and James March. *The Behavioral Theory of the Firm.* Englewood Cliffs, N.J.: Prentice Hall, 1963.
Dimock, Marshall, and Gladys Dimock. *Public Administration.* Homedale, Ill.: Dryden Press, 1969.
Downs, Anthony. *Inside Bureaucracy.* Boston: Little, Brown, 1967.
Etzioni, Amitai. *Modern Organizations.* Englewood Cliffs, N.J.: Prentice-Hall, 1964.
———. ed. *A Sociological Reader on Complex Organizations.* New York: Holt, Rinehart & Winston, 1969.
Evan, William M., ed. *Interorganizational Relations.* Philadelphia: University of Pennsylvania Press, 1978.
Evans, Frank B., and Harold T. Pinkett, eds. *Research in the Administration of Public Policy.* Washington, D.C.: Harvard University Press, 1975.
Gawthrop, Louis. *Administrative Politics and Social Change.* New York: St. Martin's Press, 1971.
Halperin, Morton H. *Bureaucratic Politics and Foreign Policy.* Washington, D.C.: Brookings Institution, 1974.
Kaufman, Herbert. *Are Government Organizations Immortal?* Washington, D.C.: Brookings Institution, 1976.
Lane, Frederick C. *Current Issues in Public Administration.* New York: St. Martin's Press, 1978.
Lawrence, Paul, and Jay Lorsch. *Organization and Environment.* Homewood, Ill.: Richard Irwin, 1969.
Levine, Robert A. *Public Planning.* New York: Basic Books, 1972.
March, James, ed. *Handbook of Organizations.* Chicago: Rand McNally, 1965.
Maurer, John G., ed. *Readings in Organization Theory.* New York: Random House, 1971.
Mintzberg, Henry. *The Nature of Managerial Work.* New York: Harper & Row, 1973.
Natemeyer, Walter E., ed. *Organizational Behavior.* Oak Park, Ill.: Moore, 1978.
Perrow, Charles. *Organizational Analysis: A Sociological View.* Belmont, Calif.: Brooks/Cole, 1970.
Pfeffer, Jeffrey, and Gerald Salancik. *The External Control of Organizations.* New York: Harper & Row, 1978.

Pugh, D. S., ed. *Organization Theory.* New York: Penguin, 1971.

Pugh, D. S., D. J. Hickson, and C. R. Hirings. *Writers on Organizations.* Middlesex, Eng.: Penguin Books, 1973.

Rainey, H. G., R. W. Backoff, and C. H. Levine. "Comparing Public and Private Organizations." *Public Administration Review* 36 (March/April 1976):233-244.

Rourke, Francis E., ed. *Bureaucratic Power in National Politics.* Boston: Little, Brown, 1978.

Schon, Donald A. *Beyond the Stable State.* New York: Norton, 1971.

Seidman, Harold. *Politics, Position, and Power.* New York: Oxford University Press, 1970.

Selznik, Philip. *Leadership in Administration.* Berkeley: University of California Press, 1957.

Shafritz, Jay M., and Albert C. Hyde, eds. *Classics of Public Administration.* Oak Park, Ill.: Moore, 1978.

Simon, Herbert. *Administrative Behavior.* New York: Free Press, 1957.

Thompson, James D. *Organizations in Action.* New York: McGraw-Hill, 1967.

Wilensky, Harold L. *Organizational Intelligence.* New York: Basic Books, 1967.

Wilson, James Q. *Varieties of Police Behavior.* New York: Atheneum, 1973.

Woll, Peter. *American Bureaucracy.* New York: W. W. Norton, 1977.

Environmental Policy

Anderson, Frederick R. *NEPA in the Courts.* Baltimore: Johns Hopkins University Press, 1973.

Armstrong, Terry R., ed. *Why Do We Still Have an Ecological Crisis?* Englewood Cliffs, N.J.: Prentice-Hall, 1972.

Bokchin, Murray. *Our Synthetic Environment.* New York: Harper & Row, 1974.

Brubaker, Sterling. *To Live on Earth.* Baltimore: Johns Hopkins University Press, 1972.

Calabresi, Guido, and Philip Bobbitt. *Tragic Choices.* New York: Norton, 1978.

Caldwell, Lynton Keith. *Environment: A Challenge to Modern Society.* Garden City, N.Y.: Doubleday, 1971.

_____ . *Man and His Environment: Policy and Administration.* New York: Harper & Row, 1975.

Canon, James. *A Clear View.* Emmans, Pa.: Rodale Press, 1975.

Committee on Environmental Decision-Making. *Decision-Making in the Environmental Protection Agency.* Washington, D.C.: National Academy of Sciences, 1977.

———. *Decision-Making in the Environmental Protection Agency: Case Studies.* Vol. 2A. Washington, D.C.: National Academy of Sciences, 1977.

———. *Decision-Making in the Environmental Protection Agency: Selected Working Papers.* Vol. 2B. Washington, D.C.: National Academy of Sciences, 1977.

Committee on National Statistics. *Environmental Monitoring.* Washington, D.C.: National Academy of Sciences, 1977.

Committee on Principles of Decision-Making for Regulatory Chemicals in the Environment. *Decision-Making for Regulatory Chemicals in the Environment.* Washington, D.C.: National Academy of Sciences, 1975.

Commoner, Barry. *The Closing Circle.* New York: Bantam Books, 1974.

———. *Science and Survival.* New York: Viking, 1966.

Council on Environmental Quality. *Environmental Quality 1970-1979 Annual Reports.* Washington, D.C.: Government Printing Office, 1979.

Crenson, Mathew. *The Unpolitics of Air Pollution.* Baltimore: Johns Hopkins University Press, 1970.

Dales, J. H. *Pollution, Property and Prices.* Toronto: University of Toronto Press, 1968.

Davies, J. Clarence III, and Barbara S. Davies. *The Politics of Pollution.* Indianapolis: Bobbs-Merrill, 1975.

Davis, Christopher P., Jeffrey Kurtock, James P. Leape, and Frank C. Magill. "The Clean Air Act Amendments of 1977: Away from Technology Forcing?" *Harvard Environmental Law Review* 2 (1977): 1-103.

Dorfman, Robert, and Nancy Dorfman, eds. *Economics of the Environment.* New York: Norton, 1972.

Downs, Anthony. "Up and Down With Ecology—The 'Issue Attention Cycle.' " *The Public Interest* 29 (March 1972):38-56.

Dubos, Rene. *Man Adapting.* New Haven, Conn.: Yale University Press, 1972.

Ehrlich, Paul, Anne Ehrlich, and John Holdren. *Human Ecology: Problems and Solutions.* San Francisco: W. H. Freeman, 1973.

Erlich, Paul, John Holdren, and Richard Holm. *Man and the Ecosphere: Readings from the Scientific American.* San Francisco: W. H. Freeman, 1971.

Environment and Natural Resources Policy Division of the Congressional Research Service of the Library of Congress. *Pollution Taxes, Effluent Charges, and Other Alternatives for Pollution Control: A Report Prepared for the Committee on Environment and Public Works, U.S. Senate.* Washington, D.C., May 1977.

Environmental Policy Division of the Congressional Research Service of the Library of Congress. *A Legislative History of the Clean Air Amendments of 1970.* Washington, D.C., January 1974.

_____ . *The Status of Environmental Economics: An Update: A Report Prepared for the Committee on Environment and Public Works, U.S. Senate.* Washington, D.C., July 1979.

Environmental Research Assessment Committee. *Effects of a Polluted Environment: Research and Development Needs.* Washington, D.C.: National Academy of Sciences, 1977.

_____ . *Fates of Pollutants.* Washington, D.C.: National Academy of Sciences, 1977.

_____ . *Sources of Residuals and Techniques for Their Control.* Washington, D.C.: National Academy of Sciences, 1977.

EPA Office of Planning and Evaluation. *Analysis of Economic Effects of Environmental Regulations on the Integrated Iron and Steel Industry.* Wellesly Hills, Mass.: Temple, Barker and Sloane, 1977.

_____ . *Economic Impacts of Pulp and Paper Industry Compliance with Environmental Regulations.* Boston: A. D. Little, 1977.

Esposito, John C. *Vanishing Air.* New York: Grossman, 1970.

Fortune Magazine Editors. *Environment: A National Mission for the Seventies.* New York: Harper & Row, 1970.

Freeman, A. Myrick III, Robert H. Haveman, and Allen V. Kneese. *The Economics of Environmental Policy.* Santa Barbara, Calif.: Wiley, 1973.

Friedlaender, Ann F. *Approaches to Controlling Air Pollution.* Cambridge, Mass.: M.I.T. Press, 1978.

Goldman, Marshall. *The Spoils of Progress: Environmental Pollution in the Soviet Union.* Cambridge, Mass.: M.I.T. Press, 1972.

Grad, Frank P., et al. *Environmental Control.* New York: Columbia University Press, 1971.

Hardin, Garret, and John Baden. *Managing the Commons.* San Francisco: W. H. Freeman, 1977.

Harrison, David. "Controlling Automotive Emissions: How to Save More than $1 Billion Per Year and Help the Poor Too." *Public Policy* 25 (1977):527.

Hays, Samuel. "Clean Air: From the 1970 Act to the 1977 Amendments." *Duquesne Law Review* 17 (1978-79):33-67.

Heilbroner, Robert L. *An Inquiry into the Human Prospect.* New York: Norton, 1975.

Henning, Daniel H. *Environmental Policy and Administration.* New York: American Elsevier, 1974.

Hirsch, Fred. *Social Limits to Growth.* Cambridge, Mass.: Harvard University Press, 1976.

Holden, Mathew, Jr. *Pollution Control As a Bargaining Process.* Ithaca, N.Y.: Cornell University Water Resources Center, 1966.

Jacoby, Henry D., John D. Steinbruner et al. *Clearing the Air: Federal Policy on Automotive Emissions Control.* Cambridge, Mass.: Ballinger, 1973.

Jaffee, Louis L., and Laurence H. Tribe. *Environmental Protection.* Chicago: Bracton Press, 1971.

Johnson, Ralph W., and Gardner M. Brown, Jr. *Cleaning Up Europe's Waters: Economics, Management, and Policies.* New York: Praeger, 1976.

Johnson, Warren. *Muddling Toward Frugality.* San Francisco: Sierra Club Books, 1978.

Jones, Charles O. *Clean Air: The Policies and Politics of Pollution Control.* Pittsburgh: University of Pittsburgh Press, 1975.

Kneese, Allen V. *Economics and the Environment.* New York: Penguin, 1977.

Kneese, Allen V., and Charles L. Schultze. *Pollution, Prices and Public Policy.* Washington, D.C.: Brookings Institution, 1975.

Koch, C. James, and Robert A. Leone. "The Clean Water Act: Unexpected Impacts on Industry." *Harvard Environmental Law Review* 3 (1979): 84-112.

Kormondy, Edward J. *Concepts of Ecology.* Englewood Cliffs, N.J.: Prentice-Hall, 1976.

———, ed. *Readings in Ecology.* Englewood Cliffs, N.J.: Prentice-Hall, 1965.

Krier, James E. *Environmental Law and Policy.* Indianapolis: Bobbs-Merrill, 1971.

Krier, James E., and Edmund Ursin. *Pollution and Policy.* Berkeley: University of California Press, 1977.

Kroch, Eugene A., and William P. Sterling. "Environmental Economics Literature of 1976: Benefit-Cost Analysis and Effluent Charges." *Harvard Environmental Law Review* 1 (1976):645-662.

Liroff, Richard A. *A National Policy for the Environment.* Bloomington: Indiana University Press, 1976.

Marcus, Alfred. "Command and Control: An Assessment of Smokestack Emission Regulation." Working Paper Series, Graduate School of Business, University of Pittsburgh, July 1978.

———. "The Disproportionate Power of Environmentalists." *Harvard Environmental Law Review* 2 (1977)1580 500.

———. "Recent Proposals to Improve Environmental Policy Making: Generalizing Institutions, Pollution Charges, and Information Management." *Harvard Environmental Law Review* 1 (1976):632-645.

Margolis, Howard. "The Politics of Auto Emissions." *Public Interest* 49 (Fall 1977):3-14.

Meadows, Donella H., Dennis L. Meadows, Jorgen Randers, and William W. Behrens III. *The Limits to Growth.* New York: Universe Books, 1972.

Nash, Roderick, ed. *The American Environment: Readings in the History of Conservation.* Reading, Mass.: Addison-Wesley, 1968.

National Academy of Sciences, National Academy of Engineering. Co-ordinating Committee on Air Quality Studies. *Air Quality and Automobile Emission Control.* Prepared for the U. S. Senate, Committee on Public Works. Washington, D.C., September 1974.

Olds, David M., John C. Unkovic, and Jeff Lewin. "Thoughts on the Role of Penalties in the Enforcement of the Clean Air and Clean Water Acts." *Duquesne Law Review* 17 (1978-79):1-33.

Olson, Mancur, and Hans H. Landsberg, eds. *The No-Growth Society.* New York: Norton, 1973.

Ophuls, William. *Ecology and the Politics of Scarcity.* San Francisco: W. H. Freeman, 1977.

O'Riordan, Timothy. "Policy-Making and Environmental Management: Some Thoughts on Processes and Research Issues." *Natural Resources Journal* 16 (January 1976):55-72.

Paulsen, David F., and Robert B. Denhardt, eds. *Pollution and Public Policy.* New York: Dodd, Mead, 1973.

Pfeffer, Jeffrey. *Development of Environmental Quality Objectives and Standards.* Washington, D.C.: Mitre Corporation, 1974.

Quarles, John. *Cleaning Up America.* Boston: Houghton Mifflin, 1976.

_____. "The Transportation Control Plans—Federal Regulation's Collision with Reality." *Harvard Environmental Law Review* 2 (1977):241-264.

Revelle, Roger, and Hans H. Landsberg. *America's Changing Environment.* Boston: Beacon Press, 1970.

Rosenbaum, Walter. *The Politics of Environmental Concern.* New York: Praeger, 1973.

Schumacher, E. F. *Small Is Beautiful.* New York: Harper & Row, 1973.

Solesbury, William. "Issues and Innovations in Environmental Policy in Britain, West Germany, and California." *Policy Analysis* 2 (1976): 1-44.

Steering Committee for Analytical Studies. *Perspectives on Technical Information for Environmental Protection.* Vol. 1 Washington, D.C.: National Academy of Sciences, 1977.

Stone, Christopher D. *Should Trees Have Standing?* Los Altos, Calif.: Wm. Kaufmann, 1974.

Thompson, Dennis L., ed. *Politics, Policy, and Natural Resources.* New York: Free Press, 1972.

U.S., House of Representatives. Subcommittee on Health and the Environment of the Committee on Interstate and Foreign Commerce. *Clean Air Act Amendments of 1977.* Washington, D.C.; 1977.

U. S., Senate. Committee on Public Works. *Clean Air Amendments of 1976.* Washington, D.C., March 29, 1976.

_____. *Nomination of Russel E. Train: Hearings.* Washington, D.C., August 1, 1973.

_____. *Nomination of William D. Ruckelshaus: Hearings.* Washington, D.C., December 1, 2, 1970.

U. S., Senate. Subcommittee on Environmental Pollution of the Committee on Environmental and Public Works. *Clean Air Act Amendments of 1977.* Washington, D.C., 1977.

————. *Federal Water Pollution Control Act Amendments of 1977, Hearings.*Washington, D.C., 1977.

Voytko, James, Kurt M. Hunciker, and Richard J. Lazarus. "The Clean Water Act and Related Developments in the Federal Water Pollution Control Program During 1977." *Harvard Environmental Law Review* 2 (1977):103-199.

Whitaker, John C. *Striking a Balance: Environment and Natural Resources Policy in the Nixon-Ford Years.* Washington, D.C.: American Enterprise Institute, 1976.

White, Lawrence. "Effluent Charges as a Faster Means of Achieving Pollution Abatement." *Public Policy* 24 (1976):111-123.

Wilson, James Q., ed. *The Metropolitan Enigma.* Garden City, N.Y.: Doubleday, 1970.

Zwick, David, and Marcy Benstock. *Water Wasteland.* New York: Grossman, 1971.

Government Regulation of Business

Ackerman, Robert W. *The Social Challenge to Business.* Cambridge, Mass.: Harvard University Press, 1975.

Adams, Walter, ed. *The Structure of American Industry.* New York: Macmillan, 1971.

Anderson, James E., ed. *Politics and Economic Policy Making.* Reading, Mass.: Addison-Wesley, 1970.

Baughman, James P., George C. Lodge, and Howard Pifer. *Environmental Analysis for Management.* Homewood, Ill.: Richard Irwin, 1974.

Bernstein, Marver. *Regulating Business by Independent Commission.* Princeton, N.J.: Princeton University Press, 1955.

Berry, Jeffrey M. "Regulations and the Legislative Process." Paper prepared for delivery at the annual meeting of the American Political Science Association, 1978.

Capron, William, ed. *Technological Change in Regulated Industries.* Washington, D.C.. Brookings Institution, 1971.

Caves, Richard. *American Industry: Structure, Conduct, Performance.* Englewood Cliffs, N.J.: Prentice-Hall, 1977.

Chamberlain, Neil W. *The Limits of Corporate Responsibility.* New York: Basic Books, 1973.

Davis, Kenneth Culp. *Discretionary Justice.* Urbana, Ill.: University of Illinois Press, 1977.

Domestic Council Review Group on Regulatory Reform. "The Challenge of Regulatory Reform." Washington, D.C.: The White House, 1977.

Epstein, Edward J. *News From Nowhere.* New York: Vintage, 1973.

Epstein, Edwin M. *The Corporation in American Politics.* Englewood Cliffs, N.J.: Prentice-Hall, 1969.

Friendly, Henry J. *The Federal Administrative Agencies: The Need for Better Definition of Standards.* Cambridge, Mass.: Harvard University Press, 1962.

Green, Mark, ed. *The Monopoly Makers.* New York: Grossman, 1973.

Hughes, Jonathan R. T. *The Governmental Habit.* New York: Basic Books, 1977.

Jacobs, Donald P., ed. *Regulating Business.* San Francisco: Institute for Contemporary Studies, 1978.

Jacoby, Neil H., ed. *The Business-Government Relationship: A Reassessment.* Santa Monica, Calif.: Goodyear, 1975.

Jaffe, Louis, and Nathaniel Nathanson. *Administrative Law.* Boston: Little, Brown, 1976.

Kahn, Alfred E. *The Economics of Regulation: Principles and Institutions.* Vols. 1 and 2. New York: Wiley, 1970.

Kemp, Kathleen. "The Structure of Municipal Economic Regulation." Paper prepared for delivery at the 1979 American Society for Public Administration National Conference.

Kolko, Gabriel. *Railroads and Regulations.* New York: Norton, 1965.

Krasnow, Erwin, and Lawrence Longley. *The Politics of Broadcast Regulation.* New York: St. Martin's Press, 1978.

Krislov, S., and L. D. Musolf, eds. *The Politics of Regulation.* Boston: Houghton Mifflin, 1964.

Leone, Robert. "The Real Costs of Regulation." *Harvard Business Review* (November/December 1977):57-66.

Lilley, William, and Edward Miller. "The New Social Regulation." *Public Interest* 47 (Spring 1977):49.

MacAvoy, Paul W., ed. *The Crisis of the Regulatory Commissions.* New York: Norton, 1970.

McConnell, Grant. *Private Power and American Democracy.* New York: Random House, 1966.

McKie, James W., ed. *Social Responsibility and the Business Predicament.* Washington, D.C.: Brookings Institution, 1974.

Mitnick, Barry. "A Comparison of Regulation by Incentive and by Directive." Working paper, School of Public Administration, Ohio State University, August 1978.

———. "A Critique of Life Cycle Theories of Regulation." Working paper, School of Public Administration, Ohio State University, February 1978.

———. "Organizing Regulation: Considerations in Regulation by Incentive and by Directive." Working paper, School of Public Administration, Ohio State University, March 1, 1977.

Nadel, Mark V. *The Politics of Consumer Protection.* Indianapolis: Bobbs-Merrill, 1971.

Neale, A. D. *The Anti-trust Laws of the USA.* Cambridge, Mass.: Cambridge University Press, 1970.

Noll, Roger G. *Reforming Regulation.* Washington, D.C.: Brookings Institution, 1971.

Noll, Roger G., Merton J. Peck, and John J. McGowan. *Economic Aspects of Television Regulation.* Washington, D.C.: Brookings Institution, 1973.

Owen, Bruce, and Ronald Braeutigam. *The Regulation Game.* Cambridge, Mass.: Ballinger, 1978.

Post, James L. *Corporate Behavior and Social Change.* Reston, Va.: Reston, 1978.

Posner, Richard A. *Economic Analysis of Law.* Boston: Little, Brown, 1977.
_____ . "Theories of Economic Regulation." *Bell Journal of Economics* 5 (Autumn 1974):335-358.

Preston, Lee, and James Post. *Private Management and Public Policy.* Englewood Cliffs, N.J.: Prentice-Hall, 1975.

Rothbard, Murray. *Power and Market.* San Francisco: Sheed Andrews, and McMeel, 1970.

Sabatier, Paul. "Social Movements and Regulatory Agencies Toward a More Adequate—and Less Pessimistic—Theory of 'Clientele Capture.' " *Policy Sciences* 6 (September 1975):301-342.

Schultze, Charles L. *The Public Use of Private Interest.* Washington, D.C.: Brookings Institution, 1977.

Shanahan, Eileen. "Government Regulation: What Kind of Reform?" Washington, D.C.: American Enterprise Institute, 1976.

Stigler, George J. *The Citizen and the State.* Chicago: University of Chicago Press, 1975.

Stone, Christopher. *Where the Law Ends.* New York: Harper & Row, 1975.

Turner, James S. *The Chemical Feast.* New York: Grossman, 1970.

U.S., House of Representatives, Ninety-fourth Congress. Subcommittee on Oversight and Investigations of the Committee on Interstate and Foreign Commerce. *Federal Regulation and Regulatory Reform.* Washington, D.C.: U.S. Government Printing Office, 1976.

U. S. Senate. Committee on Government Operations. *Regulatory Reform, Hearings.* Washington, D.C. November 21, 22, 25, 1974.

Ways, Max, ed. *The Future of Business.* New York: Pergamon, 1979.

Weaver, Suzanne. *Decision to Prosecute.* Cambridge, Mass.: M.I.T. Press, 1977.

Weidenbaum, Murray L. *Business, Government, and the Public.* Englewood Cliffs, N.J.: Prentice-Hall, 1977.

Wilcox, Clair, and William Shepherd. *Public Policies Toward Business.* Homewood, Ill.: Richard Irwin, 1975.

Wilson, James Q. "The Dead Hand of Regulation.'" *Public Interest* 25 (Fall 1971):40.

Index

ABOUT THE AUTHOR

Alfred A. Marcus is currently a policy analyst working on energy and environmental issues for the Battelle Science and Government Study Center, Seattle, Washington. His articles have appeared in *The Harvard Environmental Law Review* and *The Politics of Regulation*, edited by James Q. Wilson.